Pros and Cons: Arguing Different Points of View

by

Mark Jewel

Asahi Press

音声再生アプリ「リスニング・トレーナー」を使った音声ダウンロード

朝日出版社開発のアプリ、「リスニング・トレーナー（リストレ）」を使えば、教科書の音声をスマホ、タブレットに簡単にダウンロードできます。どうぞご活用ください。

◉ アプリ【リスニング・トレーナー】の使い方

《アプリのダウンロード》

App StoreまたはGoogle Playから「リスニング・トレーナー」のアプリ（無料）をダウンロード

App Storeは こちら▶

Google Playは こちら▶

《アプリの使い方》

① アプリを開き「コンテンツを追加」をタップ
② 画面上部に【15647】を入力しDoneをタップ

音声ストリーミング配信 〉〉〉

この教科書の音声は、右記ウェブサイトにて無料で配信しています。

https://text.asahipress.com/free/english/

Pros and Cons: Arguing Different Points of View

Illustrations and cover design by Sheryl Jewel

Foreword

The chief aim of this textbook is to familiarize students with the process of developing and expressing an opinion on a topic of current interest. The process involves the willingness both to consider the opinions of others and to argue against those opinions when appropriate. Conflicting opinions, in other words, are what bring the key points of an issue into focus. And once the key points have been made clear, the likelihood increases for finding a way to resolve the disagreement—even if the outcome does not completely satisfy everyone. The point is, unless you make your voice heard, the outcome is likely to be even less satisfactory.

The passages and exercises in the following pages break down the topics into two sides, pro and con. Often this means that the source of the disagreement will be obvious. But sometimes (as in the case of barrier-free access), disagreement arises out of different approaches to an issue on which both sides generally agree. Such cases, I believe, show the value of argumentation to what is usually called critical thinking: an attitude of continual questioning that can be expected to identify aspects of a problem that may have been overlooked in the first rush to judgment.

If there are two words to be kept in mind with respect to expressing a convincing opinion, they are "clarity" and "support." State your opinion clearly (and as soon as possible), and provide the necessary support to demonstrate that your opinion is based on objective evidence. Easy enough advice to follow, you might think. But you would be surprised at how often it is ignored. That is not to say subtlety and subjectivity are out of place. But experience has shown the effectiveness of clearly framing an argument in terms of "pro" versus "con."

Finally, a special acknowledgment goes to my daughter Sheryl for her contribution to this textbook. In addition to designing the cover and producing the illustrations that give such apt expression to each of the topics, she played an essential role not only in selecting those topics but in conducting the necessary background research and making substantive suggestions with regard to specific arguments, examples, and the content of conversations. In that respect, this textbook is very much a collaborative effort.

Contents

Pros and Cons: Arguing Different Points of View

Food Additives

Pro

Nothing to worry about

1-02

I don't mind having additives in my food. I think some people just overreact to the words "food additives." If something makes food look and taste better without affecting the health, where's the harm?

Let me ask a question. Do you like tofu? Well, an additive called "bittern" is used to make tofu solid. Bittern contains the chemical magnesium. Has that ever bothered you before? Does it bother you now? Or are you going to continue eating tofu? 5

1-03

The only thing about additives we really need to worry about is the amount we take in. Here's an example. There's a common chemical that can cause death if a person consumes more than half a gram to 1 gram 10 per kilogram of body weight. That chemical is… salt. Surprised? Too much salt and we die, but without it we also die. People hear that their food contains an additive, and right away they think that some harmful chemical has been mixed in just to improve the flavor or texture. But like salt, there's usually no reason to be afraid of small amounts. 15

1-04

The most serious danger connected with eating food is actually food poisoning. That's why most food companies add preservatives to their products —to keep them fresh. Should we take the risk of eating spoiled food rather than use preservatives? Added preservatives are especially important for storing emergency supplies. Without them, it's almost impos- 20 sible to be prepared when disaster hits.

As far as I'm concerned, the benefits of food additives are obvious. We'd be foolish to stop using them.

《 Notes 》

(l. 1) **additives:** 添加物　(l. 2) **overreact:** 過剰反応する　(l. 4) **bittern:** にがり
(l. 5) **solid:** 固形の　(l. 6) **bother:** 悩ます、困らせる　(l. 9) **take in:** （体内に）取り込む
(l. 10) **consume:** 摂取する、食べる、飲む　(l. 16) **food poisoning:** 食中毒
(l. 17) **preservatives:** （人工）保存料　(l. 18) **spoiled:** 腐った
(l. 20) **emergency supplies:** 非常用食料品　(l. 21) **disaster:** 災害
(l. 22) **as far as I'm concerned:** 私に関するかぎり　(l. 22) **obvious:** 明白な

《 Exercises 》

I Hear What You're Saying

1. What does the writer say about tofu?

a. Eating too much can damage the health.
b. A food additive is used to make it.
c. Many people dislike the taste.

2. The writer says that salt is safe

a. no matter how much of it people consume.
b. except when people consume it as a food additive.
c. unless people consume it in very large amounts.

3. Additives are useful for storing emergency supplies because they

a. prevent the supplies from spoiling.
b. keep the supplies from getting wet.
c. take up very little storage space.

Getting to the Point

1-05

Lydia: I got a rash when I used one of those cosmetics with natural ingredients.

Nao: Natural isn't always best. Some of those ingredients are really strong. And sometimes the chemicals they use to make the ingredients aren't even listed on the label.

Lydia: Like with food, you could be (   ) with an extract instead of some natural ingredient you've never heard of.

Nao: Even organic ingredients all have scientific names. You don't have to be scared of something just because it's called an additive.

Lydia: <u>Don't you get worried</u> when they say tests on animals cause problems?

Nao: Animals aren't people, you know. Are we supposed to stop eating avocados? They're poison to every other living creature except the human race.

Lydia: Hmm. I bought these vegetables because they were grown without pesticides, but look—bugs!

Nao: Those pesticide experiments are ridiculous. They give animals huge amounts of chemicals day after day—way more than they get naturally. Of course it causes problems. But it's just so unrealistic.

1. Draw a line under the word or expression in the passage that comes closest in meaning to the underlined part of the conversation.

2. Choose the best word or expression from those below to fill in the blank space in the conversation.

worn out	better off	let down

3. Complete the following sentence by adding your own **supporting idea**.

I agree that food additives are useful because ______________________

____

____.

Con

Don't gamble with your health

1-06

From now on, my goal is to avoid anything that's filled with food additives. "This additive is completely safe," you hear from scientists and food producers. But then one day, a news report comes out that it's not. It happens all the time. We just don't know what happens to the human body after people consume food additives for decades. The data simply doesn't exist.

1-07

People who say that additives are safe just because they've been used in food for years—or that essential nutrients can also be called additives—have the mistaken belief that all additives are safe. Food products these days are different from food products in the past. They contain all sorts of additives with names no ordinary person has ever heard of before. The label may tell you that the amount of an additive is safe, but it's easy to go past a safe level by consuming other products with the same additive. What's more, scientific tests never consider the effects of having different additives in your body at the same time.

1-08

Besides, food isn't the only thing that has additives. Cosmetics, for example, have chemicals that can enter the body through the skin. You probably don't even think about that happening, even though you use the cosmetics every day. And don't forget allergies. When allergens get added to food or other products without consumers knowing about it, what are consumers supposed to do? What happens to their freedom of choice?

In my opinion, we've got to do something about food additives before we reach the point of no return.

《Notes》

(l. 1) **avoid:** 避ける (l. 3) **food producer:** 食品メーカー (l. 5) **decade:** 10 年間
(l. 8) **nutrient:** 栄養素 (l. 9) **mistaken belief:** 誤った確信 (l. 19) **allergen:** アレルゲン
(l. 21) **freedom of choice:** 選択の自由 (l. 23) **got to do ~:** (~を) しなければならない
(l. 24) **the point of no return:** 引き返せないところ

《 Exercises 》

I Hear What You're Saying

1. What does the writer say about scientists and food producers?

a. They often make incorrect statements about the safety of food additives.
b. They often try to hide information about food-additive safety.
c. They often consume food additives themselves to prove their safety.

2. According to the writer, it easy for consumers to go past a safe level of food additives when they

a. ignore all the tests on combinations of additives in the body.
b. forget to read the information about additives on food labels.
c. eat different foods that happen to contain the same additives.

3. One problem mentioned about cosmetics is that

a. consumers believe that most of them contain dangerous allergens.
b. the additives they contain can pass through the skin.
c. the cheaper the cosmetics, the more additives they contain.

Getting to the Point

1-09

Marina: I'm not really worried about food additives because I always stay away from them.

Kai: You use lip gloss, don't you?

Marina: Of course I do. So what?

Kai: Well, you lick your lips when you eat, right? That means you're eating plastic. And what about toothpaste? I'll bet you don't realize how many additives you're putting in your mouth when you brush your teeth. You may think you're taking good care of yourself, but you're just being (   ). You should start paying attention.

Marina: Why are you getting so worked up over it? I've never heard about anyone having problems from additives.

Kai: Just because you haven't heard about the problems doesn't mean they don't exist. They can even change your sense of taste.

Marina: Getting used to the taste of chemical additives. Ugh. That's scary.

1. Draw a line under the word or expression in the passage that comes closest in meaning to the underlined part of the conversation.

2. Choose the best word or expression from those below to fill in the blank space in the conversation.

ignorant	suspicious	delightful

3. Complete the following sentence by adding your own **opposing idea**.

   I am against using food additives because ______________________________

   ____

   ____.

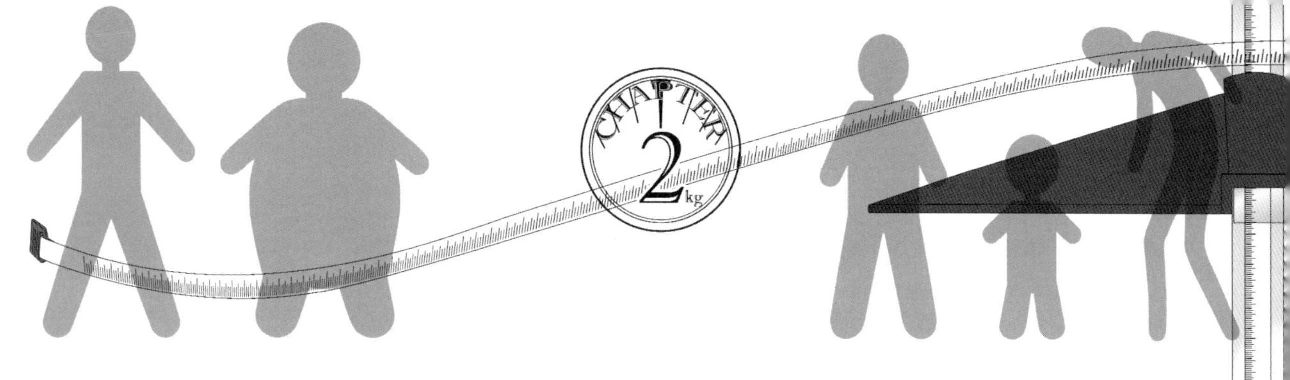

Body Image and Photoshopping

Pro

Show me at my best

1-10 Beautiful images appeal to people. In this day and age, it's only natural for advertisers to use digital editing to make their photographs more appealing. Everyone knows that the photos have been retouched, so unless there's some kind of fraud involved, I don't see the problem.

The idea is to make people pay attention, so naturally advertisers choose good-looking models—and then try to make them look better. Beauty is what people want to see. After all it's not as though advertisers make the rules. Beauty is in the eye of the beholder, they say, and in the world of advertising, it's the consumer's eye that counts. Advertisers are just trying to satisfy the consumer's idea of beauty. You can hardly blame advertisers for being good at what they do.

1-11 If you want to see people as they really are, you only have to open the door and walk outside. I get it that it's good to have models with different body types, but there's a difference between accepting people who are overweight in the real world and seeing them in ads as role models to copy. In other words, when you show overweight people in advertisements, you're sending a message that being overweight is just fine. To encourage good health, isn't it better to show models who look fit and trim, even if you have to use digital effects and CGI?

1-12 Lots of people enjoy imagining themselves as being more attractive. "Beauty is in the eye of the beholder" also means that someone can feel better about themselves by looking at a beautiful image. Advertisements make that possible, so in that way I think they actually show respect for an individual's ideal of beauty.

《 Notes 》

(l. 1) **appeal:** (人を) 引き付ける　(l. 3) **retouch:** 修正する　(l. 4) **fraud:** 詐欺
(l. 4) **be involved:** (...を) 伴う　(l. 8) **Beauty is in the eye of the beholder.:** (ことわざ) 美は見る人の基準で決まる。/美は見る人によって異なる。　(l. 10) **blame:** 非難する
(l. 13) **get it:** 理解する　(l. 14) **accept:** 受け入れる　(l. 17) **encourage:** 促進する
(l. 18) **fit and trim:** 健康ですらっとした
(l. 19) **CGI (computer-generated imagery):** コンピューター生成画像

《 Exercises 》

I Hear What You're Saying

1. The writer notes that advertisers choose models

a. according to rules that advertisers make up themselves.
b. regardless of whether the models are good-looking or not.
c. based on what advertisers think consumers will find beautiful.

2. The writer argues against using overweight models in advertisements because

a. viewers may get the wrong idea about being overweight.
b. overweight models are hard to photograph attractively.
c. people who are overweight are hard to find in the real world.

3. The writer uses the proverb "Beauty is in the eye of the beholder." to mean that

a. advertisers have a hard time understanding what consumers want to see.
b. consumers can feel beautiful when they see models who look beautiful.
c. models want advertisers to use more computer graphics in their ads.

Getting to the Point

1-13

Lydia: You know, I went into the fitting room today and saw a poster for the skirt I was going to try on. It was a big, life-size poster. The model looked stunning.

Nao: When I see a poster like that with a male model, I always feel a little embarrassed.

Lydia: (   )?

Nao: I don't know. Maybe because I know it's been photoshopped and nobody could ever look that good in real life.

Lydia: Well, it doesn't really bother me. In fact, I like seeing someone beautiful modeling the clothes I want to wear. It's good for my self-image.

Nao: What do you mean?

Lydia: I don't think the clothes are actually going to change my body or anything. But I feel confident I'm going to look my best, and other people can sense that confidence in me.

Nao: Ah, I see. In other words, it's the feeling that counts.

1. Draw a line under the word or expression in the passage that comes closest in meaning to the underlined part of the conversation.

2. Choose the best word or expression from those below to fill in the blank space in the conversation.

How come?	What now?	Why not?

3. Complete the following sentence by adding your own **supporting idea**.

I think retouched advertisements are fine because ______________________

____

____.

Con

Time to get real

1-14

All those photoshopped ads of people who don't exist in real life—it's going too far. Tricky camera angles and computer graphics used to make the models look better, and for what? The image we have of our own bodies only gets more and more unrealistic.

I mean, there's hardly anyone alive who doesn't have some kind of skin flaw. So when you see a model in a photo who seems to have perfect skin, you feel unattractive. And then you see another photo like that, and then another, and then another. It's no wonder people start taking them as their standard of beauty over real life. It's an illusion—just that and nothing more. But even so, you can't get it out of your head.

1-15

Even the models in the photographs fall under the same spell. When the photos get published, they see themselves without the little imperfections that make them who they are. And since that becomes their standard of beauty, they try even harder to match that false image. It becomes a vicious circle. Before long, they start to feel that the wrinkles that appear in their faces when they pose look strange, or that they need to go on some crazy diet to stay thin.

1-16

I'm worried that in the future, some fashion makers may even stop selling clothes in different sizes just so they can improve their brand. "Let's weed out the customers we don't really want," they'll say, and they'll start producing just one "perfect" size. More and more people would never feel happy with the way they are. I consider it a potential threat to our society.

《 Notes 》

(l. 2) **tricky:** 巧妙な (l. 5) **skin flaw:**（シミなど）肌の欠点
(l. 8) **no wonder ~:** 〜も無理はない (l. 9) **illusion:** 錯覚、幻想
(l. 11) **fall under the same spell:** 同じ魅力のとりこになる (l. 12) **imperfection:** 欠点
(l. 15) **vicious circle:** 悪循環 (l. 15) **wrinkle:** しわ (l. 16) **pose:** ポーズをとる
(l. 20) **weed out ~:** 〜を引き抜く、除外する (l. 22) **potential threat**: 潜在的脅威

《 Exercises 》

I Hear What You're Saying

1. The writer thinks that when people keep seeing photos of models with perfect skin, they

a. learn what models look like in real life.
b. start to buy more makeup than they need.
c. become unhappy with their own skin flaws.

2. According to the writer, models who see themselves in photoshopped ads think that

a. the ads ought to show more of their imperfections.
b. they should try harder to reach an unrealistic ideal.
c. more wrinkles would make them look like real models.

3. What is said to be a frightening possibility about the future?

a. Fashion makers producing just one size of clothes.
b. People starting to wear clothing of different sizes.
c. Customers paying too much for designer brands.

Getting to the Point

1-17

Marina: This model's face is so beautiful.

Kai: Do you think it's been photoshopped? Her skin is flawless.

Marina: I don't know. It does look a little too smooth, but she's probably beautiful in person, too.

Kai: But doesn't it make you think she might not look so beautiful in real life? If you keep seeing unrealistic images in ads all the time, you end up (   ) when you see the real thing. Body image is really important.

Marina: Come on. You're over-thinking it.

Kai: Or take it from the opposite side. Let's say you buy a nice outfit after seeing a model in some ad. Later, when you put it on, you can't stop thinking about the ad and keep comparing yourself with the model in your mind.

Marina: Yeah, I have to admit that's happened to me before. I thought the clothes would make me feel good about myself, but I was always thinking about the way people were looking at me. Ouch!

Kai: I feel your pain.

1. Draw a line under the word or expression in the passage that comes closest in meaning to the underlined part of the conversation.

2. Choose the best word or expression from those below to fill in the blank space in the conversation.

disillusioned	indifferent	uncommon

3. Complete the following sentence by adding your own **opposing idea**.

I am against photoshopping in photographs because ______________________

____

____.

Undergrounding

Pro

Less is more

1-18

Does anyone think that a forest of utility poles with power lines hanging between them like spiderwebs is pleasing to the eye? Moving utility lines underground is the best way to rid ourselves of such eyesores.

With expos being held in so many Japanese cities and sightseers arriving from all over the world, creating an attractive cityscape should be the number-one priority of the tourist industry. Undergrounding is the best way to preserve the historical beauty of our towns while providing all the conveniences of modern life. It's only common sense. As a matter of fact, undergrounding has increased tourism and raised land values wherever it's been. introduced.

1-19

But there's more than beauty at stake. Safety is just as important. Earthquakes and typhoons cause utility poles to fall and power lines to break, adding to the danger from those natural events. Downed utility poles and power lines also prevent access by emergency vehicles, putting even more lives at risk. Utility poles are a hazard to cars, trucks, and buses, blocking drivers' views and increasing the chances of an accident. And if you happen to hit one of these hard, rigid objects, watch out. It's not like hitting a guardrail or even another car. According to one study, the death rate from an accident rises ten times when drivers crash into a utility pole. Furthermore, it's not uncommon to hear of accidents where pedestrians get trapped between a car and a utility pole.

1-20

Undergrounding eliminates all these problems and has the benefit of adding strong protection and easy maintenance to the energy grid. Let's give ourselves more breathing space aboveground by putting more of our infrastructure underground.

《 Notes 》

(l. 2) **pleasing to the eye:** 目に訴える (l. 3) **rid oneself of ~:** ～から解放される
(l. 3) **eyesore:** 目障り (l. 5) **cityscape:** 都市の景観 (l. 6) **priority:** 優先度
(l. 11) **at stake:** 危機に瀕して (l. 13) **downed:** 倒された、落とされた
(l. 14) **put at risk:** 危険にさらす (l. 17) **rigid:** 固定した、動かない
(l. 18) **study:** 研究調査 (l. 20) **pedestrian:** 歩行者 (l. 23) **maintenance:** 維持
(l. 23) **energy grid:** 電力網 (l. 25) **infrastructure:** 基礎的施設、インフラ

《 Exercises 》

I Hear What You're Saying

1. According to the writer, one benefit of undergrounding for urban areas is that

a. history can be more fully appreciated.
b. the number of expos is likely to increase.
c. the price of land can be expected to fall.

2. What is NOT mentioned as a possible problem when a natural disaster strikes an area with utility poles?

a. Emergency vehicles might have trouble with access.
b. Fallen power lines could increase the danger to people.
c. Residents would have to find other sources of electricity.

3. Utility poles are said to increase the death rates of accidents because

a. large vehicles are usually the ones that hit them.
b. pedestrians often stand right next to them.
c. the poles themselves are so heavy and solid.

Getting to the Point

1-21

Lydia: Having a utility pole right in front of the house like this must really get in the way.

Nao: You can (   ). There's no place at all for cars or delivery trucks to stop. How is someone in a wheelchair supposed to get by?

Lydia: I'd hate having to look at power lines through the window. U-G-L-Y.

Nao: Not to mention the mess the birds make on the ground. And all those vines hanging from the power lines—isn't that dangerous? It could start a fire or something.

Lydia: Imagine coming to the window one morning and finding a workman staring you in the face. The truth is, it's a little scary to think that a utility pole like this is so easy to climb.

Nao: No way would I want one of these things next to *my* house!

1. Draw a line under the word or expression in the passage that comes closest in meaning to the underlined part of the conversation.

2. Choose the best word or expression from those below to fill in the blank space in the conversation.

say that again	look forward to that	keep that to yourself

3. Complete the following sentence by adding your own **supporting idea**.

   I am all for undergrounding because ________________________________

   ____

   ____.

Con

Hidden obstacles to success

1-22

The supposed benefits of undergrounding have been exaggerated—greatly so. It would be foolish to go ahead without considering the problems.

You might think, for instance, that narrow roads would be the best candidates for undergrounding. After all, that's where open space is most needed. But less space aboveground also means less space below ground. Power lines don't need much space, you say? Well, it's not just a matter of a few wires. Room has to be made for transformers and other necessary equipment, and pipes for gas, water, and sewage already take up a lot of that space. It's actually pretty crowded down there.

1-23

In addition, planning has to be coordinated among prefectural and local governments, electric companies, telephone companies, internet providers, and residents—a process that could take years. Experience tells us there's no doubt those plans would soon run into trouble. To take one example, an internet provider might drop out of the project because of the cost, so one entire area would be left without broadband while the rest of the prefecture—or the country—moves ahead. Talk about information inequality.

1-24

Earthquakes? The damage could actually be worse with power lines underground. You can talk about the strength of concrete all you want, but there's no guarantee against damage from ground displacement and liquefaction. And if damage does take place, locating the spot and accessing it would be much more difficult and time-consuming. You wouldn't be able to make any repairs at all if an area were flooded or covered with a thick layer of snow. Just how long are you willing to go without power if the worst happens?

No, you're never going to convince me that the trouble and expense of undergrounding is worth it.

《 Notes 》

(Title) **obstacle:** 障害物　(l. 1) **supposed:** 言われている、思われている
(l. 1) **exaggerate:** 誇張する、大げさに言う　(l. 8) **transformer:** 変圧器
(l. 11) **coordinate:** 調整する　(l. 11) **prefectural:** 県の
(l. 17) **talk about ~:** ～どころではない　(l. 21) **ground displacement:** 地中変異、地盤変位
(l. 22) **liquefaction:** 液状化　(l. 26) **the worst:** 最悪（の場合）
(l. 27) **convince:** 納得させる　(l. 28) **worth it:** それだけの価値はある

《 Exercises 》

I Hear What You're Saying

1. Narrow roads are said to be unsuitable for undergrounding because

a. power lines are too big to fit under them.
b. too little free space exists below them.
c. too many people use them every day.

2. According to the writer, information inequality could be caused by

a. the local government having no planning experience.
b. residents moving away to live in other neighborhoods.
c. an internet provider refusing to pay for undergrounding.

3. One point mentioned in connection with earthquakes is that

a. underground damage can be difficult to locate and repair.
b. cold weather increases the damage to underground power lines.
c. floods cause more underground damage than ground displacement.

Getting to the Point

1-25

Marina: Did you hear? They're going to bury all the power lines on our street. Now we won't have to worry so much about car and bicycle accidents.

Kai: Yeah, well, they use the utility poles for streetlights, too, remember. And then there are all those street signs and address plates. You can bet they'll be putting up some new poles for those things.

Marina: Hmm, I hadn't thought of that. Maybe things won't be so different after all.

Kai: Another thing—there are ground wires up there protecting people from lightning strikes. Those will be gone, too.

Marina: Lightning? Yikes. I don't really want to (   ) safety for convenience. I guess it's not as simple as I thought it was.

Kai: You've got to look at the big picture if you want to get a clear idea of what's going to change.

1. Draw a line under the word or expression in the passage that comes closest in meaning to the underlined part of the conversation.

2. Choose the best word or expression from those below to fill in the blank space in the conversation.

delay	sacrifice	investigate

3. Complete the following sentence by adding your own **opposing idea**.

I oppose undergrounding because ______________________________

____

____.

Do We Need the Olympics?

Pro

More than just a sports festival

1-26 It's fantastic to have an event every four years where people come together from all over the world. Cities everywhere should welcome the chance to host the Olympic Games.

In the Olympics, athletes compete against the best in the world in a wide variety of sports. They have the opportunity to set new records and achieve lifelong goals. For them, it's a chance to shine. Winning a medal in the Olympic games is like a dream come true. 5

1-27 Not only that, the Games are broadcast worldwide, so viewers can share in the excitement. Since there are so many events, it gives them the chance to learn about new and unfamiliar sports. This motivates them to take part in sports themselves, so people become healthier and more active. And when people get involved in sports, they meet other people from the same community and make new friends. It's not just about keeping healthy. Also, don't forget that that the Paralympics are held right after the Olympics. They offer the same opportunities to athletes with disabilities, and they're just as inspiring as the Olympics. 10 15

1-28 When the Olympics and Paralympics are held, new stadiums and other sports facilities are built. New businesses start up and public transportation is upgraded even before the Games begin. After the Games, local residents continue to benefit from all these improvements. Even the Olympic Villages, where the athletes stay, are converted into housing for local residents and hostels for visitors. People in other countries watch the Games or read about them and want to travel to the host country. As a 20 result, the entire country can look forward to a long-lasting economic boost. 25

Inspiration, health, new friends, and economic benefits—what more could you ask for?

《 Notes 》

(l. 3) **host:** 主催する (l. 4) **athlete:** スポーツ選手 (l. 6) **achieve:** 達成する、実現する
(l. 9) **event:** 種目 (l. 10) **motivate:** 動機を与える
(l. 12) **get involved in ~:** ～に関与する、打ち込む (l. 14) **hold:** 開催する
(l. 16) **inspiring:** 感激させる (l. 18) **facilities:** 施設
(l. 19) **upgrade:** 水準を上げる、改善する (l. 21) **convert:** (用途などを) 変更する、改造する
(l. 24) **look forward to ~:** ～を期待する (l. 25) **boost:** 後押し

《 Exercises 》

I Hear What You're Saying

1. According to the writer, athletes at the Olympic Games enjoy

a. playing sports in the warm summer weather.
b. watching other athletes win Olympic medals.
c. reaching goals they always hoped to reach.

2. Viewers of the Olympics are said to

a. pay a lot of money to watch the Games.
b. take an interest in unfamiliar events.
c. invite athletes to stay at their homes.

3. The writer notes that the economic benefits of hosting the Olympics

a. last long after the Games have ended.
b. go to visitors rather than to local residents.
c. start as soon as athletes arrive in the host country.

Getting to the Point

1-29

Lydia: I don't usually watch sports, but it's pretty amazing to see top athletes in action. And some of the new Olympic events look really exciting. Skateboarding, for instance.

Nao: That's really popular now. Why don't you (   )?

Lydia: Maybe I will. Who knows? It might be a good way to make some friends.

Nao: Sports is a great way to <u>reach out to your neighbors</u>.

Lydia: Hey, maybe I could even post videos of myself online.

Nao: And if you mention the Olympics, people from all over the world will want to add comments.

Lydia: Yeah—it'd be like having a conversation with all kinds of interesting new people.

1. Draw a line under the word or expression in the passage that comes closest in meaning to the underlined part of the conversation.

2. Choose the best word or expression from those below to fill in the blank space in the conversation.

give it a try	leave it alone	take it away

3. Complete the following sentence by adding your own **supporting idea**.

I think the Olympics are worthwhile because ______________________________

____

____.

Con

We have better things to do with our money

1-30

It may seem obvious, but who needs the Olympics when we already have so many other major international sports events? They're in the news every single day.

1-31

To begin with, there's the problem of cost. The Games just keep getting bigger and bigger, and governments keep paying more and more to host them. One thing that especially worries me is the possibility of a natural disaster happening at the same time as the Olympics. Everyone knows that disasters have been on the rise recently because of climate change and growing seismic activity. If a natural disaster hits around the time of the Olympics, how will the government find the money and manpower for relief operations and reconstruction? Workers will all be busy on Olympic projects, and the budget will have already been spent on making life better in the host city. Outer areas will just be ignored and won't get the help they need. And don't forget that all those new stadiums and other facilities have to be maintained once the Games are over. Even if no emergency takes place, taxpayers end up paying for the Olympics for years afterward.

1-32

As for the Games themselves, what a mess! Heavy traffic and tourists everywhere. Delivery services unable to make deliveries on time. Streets blocked off so marathons can be run. Trains so crowded you can hardly move. No vacancies at hotels anywhere in the host city. Sky-high prices at restaurants—if you can even get a reservation. It's more than I could take. If I lived anywhere near the host city, I'd want to take a long vacation somewhere nice and quiet.

In today's world, the Olympics are a waste of a country's resources. It's time for us to admit that the Olympics just aren't worth it anymore.

《 Notes 》

(l. 6) **natural disaster:** 自然災害　(l. 8) **on the rise:** 上昇して、増加して
(l. 9) **seismic activity:** 地震活動　(l. 10) **manpower:** 人的資源、マンパワー
(l. 11) **relief operations:** 救済活動　(l. 12) **the budget:** （国などの）予算
(l. 13) **ignore:** 無視する　(l. 15) **maintain:** 維持する　(l. 16) **taxpayers:** 納税者
(l. 17) **mess:** 乱雑、ゴチャゴチャ　(l. 20) **vacancy:** 空室　(l. 24) **resources:** 資源
(l. 25) **admit:** 認める　(l. 25) **be worth it:** それだけの価値がある

《 Exercises 》

I Hear What You're Saying

1. Which of the following is said to be a possible outcome of a natural disaster around the time of the Olympics?

a. The host city for the Olympics might have to be moved.
b. Climate change could quickly increase in speed.
c. Workers for rebuilding would be hard to find.

2. The writer says that after the Olympics, taxpayers have to pay to

a. continue operating the new facilities that were built.
b. remove all the unnecessary buildings that were put up.
c. replace the Olympic stadium with more useful buildings.

3. The writer mentions wanting to take a vacation to emphasize

a. the excitement of living in an Olympic host city.
b. the unpleasantness of city life during the Olympics.
c. the high cost of traveling overseas during the Games.

Getting to the Point

1-33

Marina: Well, here I am, back in Japan in time for the Olympics. It's such an exciting event. I'm thinking of going to check out the new stadium tomorrow.

Kai: But won't it be crowded? And it's right in the middle of summer, too. It's going to be hot.

Marina: Don't worry, <u>I can handle it</u>.

Kai: It's not just the heat, you know. With so many people around, you have to worry about catching something. Think of all the viruses floating around.

Marina: Hmm. Now that you mention it, it does make me feel a little ( ). I don't want to catch anything, and I wouldn't want people to catch something from me, either.

Kai: Lots of adults these days never got protected against diseases when they were children. If you catch something, it's off to the hospital with you. You have health insurance, right?

Marina: You know, maybe I should just stay home and watch the Games on television.

1. Draw a line under the word or expression in the passage that comes closest to having the opposite meaning of the underlined part of the conversation.

2. Choose the best word or expression from those below to fill in the blank space in the conversation.

fortunate	anxious	stubborn

3. Complete the following sentence by adding your own **opposing idea**.

I am against holding the Olympics because ______________________________

____

____.

Mobile Ads

Pro

Something for nothing

1-34

I don't want to pay for the information I get online. Who does? Mobile ads make it easy to get information over the internet for free, so I don't have anything bad to say about them.

With the number of web services growing, it hurts to have to pay for each and every one. Offer something for free by showing an ad, though, and the customers start coming. The more visitors you get, the more money you make, and basically everyone's happy. Not only that, the profit from the ads makes it possible to improve the service you're providing.

1-35

Now, of course an advertiser is going to want to grab a potential customer's attention by putting the ads where they get noticed: front and center. And viewers have to wait for the commercials to end before they can watch a video. That can't be helped—everyone understands it's part of the deal. The important thing is to make a strong impact so that viewers take an interest in the service you offer. That way, business is sure to grow.

1-36

From the user's standpoint, ads make it possible to discover new services without wasting much effort. Just launch an app like always, and there it is—an instant doorway to something useful or entertaining, or both. There's a good possibility you'll find a service so useful you'll wonder how you ever managed without it. From that point of view, there's no question that mobile ads are a win-win proposition.

《 Notes 》

(l. 9) **grab attention:** 強く注意を引く (l. 10) **front and center:** 最も目立つところ、目の真ん前
(l. 13) **deal:** 取り引き、代償 (l. 16) **launch:** 立ち上げる、開く (l. 16) **app:** アプリ
(l. 19) **manage without ~:** ～なしで済ます (l. 20) **proposition:** 事柄

《 Exercises 》

I Hear What You're Saying

1. According to the writer, how can online advertisers improve the services they offer?

a. By earning money from showing their ads.
b. By charging viewers for watching their ads.
c. By paying websites to make their ads.

2. What is NOT mentioned as a possible disadvantage of mobile ads?

a. Delays when watching videos.
b. Attention-grabbing ad placement.
c. Large amounts of useless information.

3. The advantage for internet users is said to be that they can

a. be the first ones to watch new ads.
b. find new services quickly and easily.
c. see the same ads when using new apps.

Getting to the Point

1-37

Lydia: Take a look at this app I found a week or so ago. I just happened to see an ad for it, and now I use it all the time.

Nao: Cool. Ads can really be useful that way.

Lydia: Actually, I've been getting a lot of new apps through ads that come up in other apps.

Nao: There must be a lot of apps like that now. I haven't been paying much attention to the ads—maybe I've been (   ). Let me have a look.

Lydia: This one makes it easy to send photos to cloud storage, saving space on my phone.

Nao: Hey, that's convenient.

Lydia: I've got other apps that help me get work done faster, and one of them even lets me practice my French. The ads keep me up to date on the latest information, and I can even register for new games before they come out.

Nao: And all without <u>spending too much of your time</u> searching for it yourself. Wow.

1. Draw a line under the word or expression in the passage that comes closest in meaning to the underlined part of the conversation.

2. Choose the best word or expression from those below to fill in the blank space in the conversation.

giving up	missing out	rushing in

3. Complete the following sentence by adding your own **supporting idea**.

My view is that mobile ads are helpful because ______________________________

____

____.

Con

A great way to lose customers

1-38

Who really thinks mobile ads are necessary? Put up with in-your-face ads as long as some service is free? I don't think so.

Mobile ads really do seem to be taking over recently. A lot of times I have trouble telling where an ad ends and the regular content begins. Some ads play it sneaky and try to trick you into clicking on them. If you do, watch out—you'll never get back to the original page. And on smartphones, with their small screens, the ads block out everything else and just get in the way. Advertisers post the ads to get our attention, but for most of us it's such a turnoff. Give me a break.

1-39

It gets worse, of course. Some ads have nothing to do with the webpage or app where they appear, and the content can be completely inappropriate. To take an example, you may be reading a blog or using an app for users of all ages, and suddenly you get hit with an ad with an adult rating. It's disgusting, frankly, and it borders on fraud. We need to put limits on ads that force you to see things you really don't want to see. Online browsing won't be safe until they are.

1-40

Maybe someday advertisers will get the balance between convenience and irritation right. It would certainly make internet users happier. But I'm not very optimistic, and I always do my best not to play their game.

《 Notes 》

(l. 1) **put up with ~:** ～に我慢する　(l. 1) **in-your-face:** 大胆不敵な、挑発的な
(l. 3) **take over:** 優勢になる、制覇する
(l. 5) **play it sneaky:** 卑劣の行為をする、ずるいことをする
(l. 5) **trick into doing ~:** （人を）だまして～をさせる　(l. 9) **turnoff:** 興ざめさせるもの
(l. 11) **inappropriate:** 不適切　(l. 14) **disgusting:** うんざりさせる、実にいやな
(l. 14) **frankly:** 率直に（言って）　(l. 14) **border on ~:** ～まがい
(l. 18) **irritation:** いらだち、立腹　(l. 19) **optimistic:** 楽観的

《 Exercises 》

I Hear What You're Saying

1. One example given of the way mobile ads work is that they

a. force internet users to pay money to find new services.
b. make internet users think that ads are not really ads.
c. are hard for internet users to see on smartphone screens.

2. The writer is disgusted by some ads because they

a. can only be seen after you have paid for the service.
b. have no connection with the content on the original site.
c. appear only on the most popular websites and blogs.

3. The writer uses the phrase "not very optimistic" to express the idea that

a. mobile ads will probably continue to be irritating in the future.
b. internet users have started to enjoy clicking on mobile ads.
c. advertisers already know the best way to balance convenience and irritation.

Getting to the Point

1-41

Marina: Oh, come on!

Kai: What is it?

Marina: I started to watch this video, and an ad popped up at full volume. What am I supposed to do about it? And it's using up my battery, too.

Kai: Yeah, I know. Those ads run on and on, and you can't skip them. It's so annoying.

Marina: Right in the middle of the screen, covering everything. And the close button is so tiny I can barely see it.

Kai: Well, of course. And if you make the mistake of clicking on the ad, you'll find yourself on a completely different site.

Marina: I'm installing an ad blocker right away.

Kai: Advertisers just don't seem to get it. If no one wants to watch their ads, then all that effort simply (   ).

1. Draw a line under the word or expression in the passage that comes closest in meaning to the underlined part of the conversation.

2. Choose the best word or expression from those below to fill in the blank space in the conversation.

goes for nothing	makes up for everything	turns out for the best

3. Complete the following sentence by adding your own **opposing idea**.

There is no place for mobile advertisements because ______________________

____

____.

CHAPTER 6

SIM-Free Smartphones

Pro

The sooner the better

1-42

Why is it taking so long for Japanese to switch to SIM-free smartphones? With SIM-free, you don't get tied to ridiculously long contracts and can change to a new model whenever you want. Best of all, your monthly charges go way down. Even if the phone itself is more expensive to buy, the lower charges mean that the longer you use your phone, the cheaper it gets. The budget carriers use the same infrastructure as the majors, so it's not as though the quality is affected.

1-43

Another advantage is how easy tethering becomes. There's no need to go hunting for a Wi-Fi hotspot—just link your device with your smartphone and boom, you're on the net. That's all there is to it. No fuss, no wires, no worries about other people listening in. You'll wonder how you ever put up with the inconvenience of a locked phone.

1-44

Traveling abroad is where SIM-free really shines. All you have to do is buy a local SIM card and switch it with your usual one. SIM cards can be found pretty much anywhere, and most let you make voice calls as well as connect all your devices to the net. No more reading through the details of your Japanese smartphone contract to learn how to make everything work—or finding out there's no way to make things work at all.

My advice is to save yourself some headaches and keep more of your hard-earned cash in your pocket by making the move to SIM-free.

《 Notes 》

(l. 2) **ridiculously:** ばかばかしいほど (l. 2) **contract:** 契約 (l. 3) **charges:** 料金
(l. 4) **way down:** うんと下がって (l. 6) **carrier:** 通信事業者、キャリア
(l. 8) **tethering:** テザリング (l. 10) **fuss:** 余計な面倒さ
(l. 11) **listen in:** 盗聴する、立聞きする (l. 11) **put up with:** 耐える、我慢する
(l. 13) **shine:** 秀でる (l. 15) **voice call:** 音声通話 (l. 20) **hard-earned:** 苦労して稼いだ

《 Exercises 》

I Hear What You're Saying

1. The writer says that with SIM-free phones,

a. new phones are cheaper to buy and cheaper to use.
b. lower monthly charges bring down the overall cost.
c. the infrastructure is better than that of the major carriers.

2. Which of the following is said to be a benefit of SIM-free tethering?

a. You can use Wi-Fi hotspots.
b. Tethering can be handled wirelessly.
c. Other people can listen to your conversations.

3. When using a SIM-free phone overseas,

a. local SIM cards are easy to find and buy.
b. voice calls normally become hard to make.
c. your usual SIM card will work just as it is.

Getting to the Point

1-45

Lydia: Switching to a prepaid SIM card was a great idea. For one thing, it keeps me from overspending.

Nao: I imagine it'll be really convenient if you travel abroad. You won't have to deal with currency conversion or being charged for overseas calls.

Lydia: There's no contract to sign, either, so I can change providers or plans anytime I want. And if I buy a new SIM-free phone, I just pop in the same SIM card and I'm good to go. <u>Nothing could be easier</u>.

Nao: Yeah, paying a flat fee with no hidden charges certainly sounds hard to resist. I'm surprised more people don't (   ) of it.

Lydia: Personally, I like being able to recharge the SIM at a convenience store or even online. It sure beats having to go to the phone store myself.

Nao: Especially when the nearest one is half an hour away!

1. Draw a line under the word or expression in the passage that comes closest in meaning to the underlined part of the conversation.

2. Choose the best word or expression from those below to fill in the blank space in the conversation.

take advantage	have enough	get rid

3. Complete the following sentence by adding your own **supporting idea**.

Going SIM-free is a good idea because ______________________________

____

____.

Con

The grass is always greener...

1-46 So you think going SIM-free is such a great deal? You might want to think twice about that.

Discount carriers are called MVNOs, for "mobile virtual network operators." There's a reason for the "virtual"—they don't actually own the equipment. It's pretty easy to start up an MVNO by leasing equipment from 5 a major carrier, but it's also pretty easy to go out of business. And, of course, an MVNO can't really guarantee the speed or quality of the connection—the major carriers control that. I don't know about you, but I trust the people who own the equipment to deliver better quality.

1-47 As for cost, sure, your basic monthly fee may go down with SIM-free, 10 but you'll pay full price for your phone, and right now there aren't that many models to choose from. That means you'll probably have to compromise on features like cameras or wireless charging, and if the phone stops working, you may have to buy another one a lot sooner than you expected. Everyone knows that the major carriers have special campaigns that lower 15 the price of their phones, so all you have to do is wait for one of those. And then you can always count on getting good customer support.

1-48 With an MVNO, by the way, it's pretty easy to go over your data limit if you don't keep an eye on your usage. Then you have to pay extra. And the discount carriers may advertise "unlimited-use" plans, but there's a hidden 20 trap. So many people choose the unlimited-use plan that the speed goes way down. What they really mean is "unlimited as long as you don't mind slow speeds." Paying more for a so-called high-speed option doesn't help—after using two or three gigabytes of data, you'll get throttled down because of congestion. Finally, unless your plan is prepaid, many MVNOs will still 25 tie you to a contract. Then, even if you buy a cheap SIM card overseas, you're still paying your usual monthly fee. That sort of defeats the purpose, doesn't it?

All in all, you're better off without SIM-free.

《 Notes 》

(l. 3) **MVNO:** 仮想移動体通信事業者　(l. 5) **lease:** 契約で賃貸する、リースする
(l. 12) **compromise:** 妥協する　(l. 13) **feature:** 機能　(l. 13) **wireless charging:** 無線充電
(l. 17) **count on ~:** ～を頼りにする、当てにする
(l. 19) **keep an eye on ~:** ～に目をつける、～に気を付ける　(l. 23) **so-called:** いわゆる
(l. 24) **throttle down:** （速度を）絞る　(l. 25) **congestion:** 混雑
(l. 27) **defeat the purpose:** 目的にそぐわない、元も子もない　(l. 29) **all in all:** 総じて言えば
(l. 29) **be better off without ~:** ～のないほうがましだ

《 Exercises 》

I Hear What You're Saying

1. **1.** The writer does not trust the quality of MVNO service because

a. major carriers refuse to let MVNOs use their equipment.
b. MVNOs use equipment that the major carriers own.
c. the equipment used by MVNOs is old and out of date.

2. The writer mentions smartphone cameras to suggest that

a. major-carrier smartphones have better features than SIM-free smartphones.
b. SIM-free smartphones break down sooner than major-carrier smartphones.
c. both SIM-free smartphones and major-carrier smartphones take poor photographs.

3. According to the writer, the unlimited-use data plans offered by MVNOs

a. actually offer users only two or three gigabytes of data usage.
b. are only available to users who buy their SIM cards overseas.
c. are so popular that data speeds are limited even with a high-speed option.

Getting to the Point

1-49

Marina: Recently I've been wondering if I should go SIM-free.

Kai: Why's that? Don't you use your smartphone that much?

Marina: No, I do, I do. Even if I switch, I'd want to keep uploading photos and videos to social media and log in to my favorite games every day.

Kai: Do you have any idea what your data usage is? It sounds to me like you might end up paying even more with an MVNO. It'd be a real (   ) to keep recharging your SIM card all the time.

Marina: Hmm. I remember asking for a pretty big plan, and I do have a high-speed connection. I have to admit I haven't compared the different plans very carefully.

Kai: Well, that's just it—<u>you seem to be rushing into things</u>. You're probably better off with what you've already got.

1. Draw a line under the word or expression in the passage that comes closest in meaning to the underlined part of the conversation

2. Choose the best word or expression from those below to fill in the blank space in the conversation.

reward	absence	bother

3. Complete the following sentence by adding your own **opposing idea**.

I have problems with going SIM-free because ______________________________

____

____.

100-Yen Shops

Pro

Luxury on the cheap

1-50 Why criticize stores that do so much for consumers of limited means? These consumers need to keep an eye on every yen they spend, so if 100-yen shops didn't exist, their lives would become even harder.

The stores work hard to keep costs low for consumers. Selling everything at a fixed price of 100 yen brings in shoppers, so the stores don't have to spend a lot on advertising. No troublesome planning for bargain sales, no special marketing skills to be mastered, and employees can be hired at relatively low wages. Cutting these operating costs is a real advantage when it comes to the stores' bottom line. What's more, the stores purchase their stock in bulk, which really brings the buying price down. This gives them a bigger margin to work with than most regular retail stores, so reducing prices becomes even easier.

1-51 And is it necessary to mention the huge variety of merchandise you can find? Household goods, snacks, stationery, clothing, even souvenirs—all just a few steps from the street or sidewalk. The fact is, many 100-yen-shop customers aren't just trying to save money, they're taking advantage of the convenience of being able to walk in, grab some small item they need, and walk right back out again. It's hardly surprising that now in Japan, there are actually more 100-yen shops than convenience stores!

1-52 The economy as a whole benefits as much as individual consumers. Sales are strong and growing, and jobs are easy to find. Despite the low wages and pressure on other retail stores, there's no question they're making a positive contribution to the economy. Lots of the merchandise is manufactured domestically, and for the items that aren't, well, even that has a positive side. Let me put it this way: it's not that Japan is losing manufacturing to other countries, it's more like Japan is providing those countries with the chance to develop their own manufacturing sector. It's sort of like the saying "Give a man a fish, and you feed him for a day. Teach a man to fish, and you feed him for a lifetime." 25

《 Notes 》

(Title) **on the cheap:** 安く (l. 1) **of limited means:** 資力の乏しい
(l. 2) **keep an eye on ~:** 〜に気を付ける (l. 7) **marketing skills:** 販売技能
(l. 8) **wages:** 賃金 (l. 9) **bottom line:** 最終損益 (l. 9) **in bulk:** 大量に
(l. 10) **margin:** 利鞘、マージン (l. 11) **retail store:** 小売店 (l. 13) **merchandise:** 商品
(l. 14) **stationery:** 文房具 (l. 17) **grab:** 素早くとる (l. 23) **domestically:** 国内で
(l. 24) **positive:** 肯定的な (l. 27) **manufacturing sector:** 産業部門
(l. 27) **saying:** ことわざ、格言

《 Exercises 》

I Hear What You're Saying

1. Hundred-yen shops are said to be able to lower consumer prices by

a. paying less than other stores to buy their merchandise.
b. hiring outside companies to do their advertising.
c. having their own workers plan the stores' bargain sales.

2. Which of the following is said to be true of 100-yen-shop customers?

a. They get a lot of exercise walking to the shops.
b. They like being able to buy merchandise quickly.
c. They prefer to shop at convenience stores instead.

3. One reason given for the way the Japanese economy benefits from 100-yen shops is that

a. employees are happy to work for low wages.
b. sales overseas are increasing rapidly.
c. more jobs are available for workers to fill.

Getting to the Point

1-53

Lydia: A hundred-yen shop opened near the station, so I feel like I hit the jackpot. Now I don't have to go online just to buy some of the small things I need.

Nao: With prices going up so much recently, having a hundred-yen shop close by <u>is a big plus</u>.

Lydia: A few days ago, I was able to buy something for a hundred yen that had a price sticker on it for over a thousand yen.

Nao: Wow. That probably means it's leftover merchandise, but at least it gets sold that way, and for us shoppers, it's a bargain.

Lydia: And when you're inside the store, you can (   ) lots of other things you need at the same time.

Nao: I know that's how it is for me. I always end up with more than I planned to buy when I walked in. I probably spend more at hundred-yen shops than I do anywhere else!

1. Draw a line under the word or expression in the passage that comes closest in meaning to the underlined part of the conversation.

2. Choose the best word or expression from those below to fill in the blank space in the conversation.

load up on	walk out on	look down on

3. Complete the following sentence by adding your own **supporting idea**.

I am in favor of 100-yen shops because ______________________________

____

____.

Con

Save now, pay later

1-54 Everyone thinks of 100-yen shops as some kind of amazing innovation, but what they're really doing is slowly eating away at our social fabric.

It's shortsighted to keep selling cheap merchandise just because consumers are trying to hold back on their spending. Unless you keep the long run in mind, the economy will come sputtering to a stop. Prices rise 5 in the distribution channel because of the expenses and labor costs added as products gradually move from suppliers to the retail shelves. As a result, workers' incomes go up, and spending increases. Keep wages down, however, and workers' incomes drop. They have less money to spend, and resistance to buying only increases. This means that raising workers' wages 10 should be our first priority. But hundred-yen shops go in the opposite direction and pay low wages to part-timers. The owners don't seem to realize that they're digging their own graves as far as the economy goes.

1-55 Here's what can happen. Let's say a 100-yen shop opens up in a neighborhood, creating 10 new jobs. Shoppers start coming to the store because 15 of the low prices, taking business away from other stores in the same area. Before long, those stores fail, and all the jobs they provided—much more than 10—disappear. Not only that, since the stores fail, the neighborhood becomes less appealing to potential new residents because it doesn't seem so attractive anymore. What seemed like a promising beginning reaches a 20 disappointing end.

1-56 There's no way to escape a deflationary spiral when prices have already started to collapse. Businesses like 100-yen shops can continue to make money, but if profits aren't reinvested in wages, the only positive effect is a small increase in the level of personal spending. Society loses more than 25 it gains. The lesson is clear: Let your attention get distracted by a mountain of cheap goods, and you'll end up having the rug pulled out from under you.

《**Notes**》

(l. 1) **innovation:** 新機軸、革新、イノベーション　(l. 2) **eat away at ~:** ～を侵食する
(l. 2) **social fabric:** 社会組織　(l. 3) **shortsighted:** 近視眼的、目先のことしか考えないような
(l. 4) **hold back on ~:** ～を控える、～を渋る　(l. 4) **the long run:** 長期間
(l. 5) **sputtering:** プッスンプッスンと音を立てながら
(l. 6) **distribution channel:** 流通経路　(l. 6) **labor costs:** 労働賃金
(l. 7) **retail shelves:** 店頭　(l. 9) **resistance:** 抵抗　(l. 11) **priority:** 優先順位
(l. 13) **dig one's own grave:** 自分で自分の首を絞める　(l. 18) **fail:** 倒産する
(l. 19) **appealing:** 魅力的な　(l. 20) **promising:** 将来有望な
(l. 20) **disappointing:** 失望的な　(l. 22) **deflationary spiral:** デフレの悪循環
(l. 23) **collapse:** 崩壊する　(l. 24) **reinvest:** 再投資する　(l. 26) **distract:** 散らす、逸らす
(l. 27) **have the rug pulled out from under one:** （人の）足をすくわれる

《 Exercises 》

I Hear What You're Saying

1. The reason given for the shortsightedness of selling cheap merchandise is that

a. paying low wages reduces consumers' willingness to spend money.
b. the distribution channel becomes too long for suppliers to manage.
c. part-timers will eventually stop working for wages that are too low.

2. Which of the following is NOT mentioned as a possible outcome of a 100-yen shop opening in a neighborhood?

a. Residents refusing to buy merchandise at the shop.
b. The overall number of jobs becoming smaller.
c. The neighborhood seeming less attractive to outsiders.

3. According to the writer, business at 100-yen shops cannot really help during deflation because the shops

a. end up spending much more money than they make.
b. have more merchandise for sale than consumers can buy.
c. are more interested in making money than in paying their workers.

Getting to the Point

1-57

Marina: You can find the same thing at a hundred-yen shop, can't you? Why not buy it there?

Kai: You know, that's exactly why so many stores are going out of business. People think that if they can get something easily for a hundred yen, there's no reason to (   ) to buy it somewhere else.

Marina: But for the buyer, cheaper is better, right? Paying more is <u>the last thing they want</u>.

Kai: Yeah, but that's only on the surface. People work hard to make and deliver all of those things, but they don't get much in return for their efforts when the price is so low. I really feel I should be paying more than a hundred yen for most of that stuff.

Marina: I guess for manufacturers it's better to have lots of orders than get stuck with unsold merchandise, but the low prices they get paid must make it tough. If hundred-yen shops didn't exist, they could set more reasonable prices.

Kai: Now I think you're getting it. It's all about being able to make a fair profit.

1. Draw a line under the word or expression in the passage that comes closest to having the opposite meaning of the underlined part of the conversation.

2. Choose the best word or expression from those below to fill in the blank space in the conversation.

make the most of their time	take advantage of their position
go out of their way	

3. Complete the following sentence by adding your own **opposing idea**.

Having too many 100-yen shops is unacceptable to me because ________

____

____.

Barrier-Free Everywhere?

Pro

Access for all

1-58 Barrier-free—the freer the better. I can't believe that anyone these days would be against making it possible for more people to live lives that are safer and more meaningful.

Some people worry about the effect barrier-free has on the appearance and atmosphere at Japanese historical sites, but you can't expect appearances to stay the same over time. To take one example, electric lights are used to light up castles and other Japanese historical buildings at night. Who thinks that we should keep castles dark at night because they didn't have electricity in premodern times? In the same way, barrier-free remodeling simply reflects modern circumstances. Accepting change doesn't mean we're denying the past. Rather, it helps make the past meaningful for those of us living in the present.

1-59 If we think it's important to experience history directly, then it's important to give everyone the chance to do so. At the most basic level, that means adding things like slopes and handrails. Protective mats can be put on floors to prevent damage from wheelchairs, and tenji blocks should be installed to help people with visual impairments. The benefits of improving access far outweigh the minor effect on appearance.

1-60 Elevators and other major renovations may need more careful planning. But it's easy to overlook the fact that many of Japan's existing castles only look old on the outside. The inside doesn't look like the interior of a castle at all. Has that ruined the experience for visitors? Some of the castles are even made of concrete. Is it possible to recreate history using concrete? If so—and I think it *is* possible—surely an elevator can be installed inside a castle without damaging the historical atmosphere.

How are people supposed to appreciate their cultural heritage if they're prevented from experiencing it firsthand? There's no reason to waste time making that heritage accessible to everyone.

《 **Notes** 》

(l. 4) **appearance:** 風景　(l. 5) **atmosphere:** 雰囲気　(l. 9) **premodern:** 前近代
(l. 9) **remodeling:** 改造、改装　(l. 10) **reflect:** 反映する　(l. 11) **deny:** 否定する
(l. 11) **rather:** むしろ　(l. 15) **handrail:** 手すり　(l. 16) **tenji block:** 点字ブロック
(l. 17) **install:** 設置する、取り付ける　(l. 17) **visual impairment:** 視覚障害
(l. 18) **outweigh ~:** ～より重要である　(l. 20) **overlook:** 見過ごす　(l. 21) **interior:** 内部
(l. 22) **ruin:** 台無しにする　(l. 23) **recreate:** 再現する　(l. 24) **surely:** 間違いなく
(l. 26) **appreciate:** 真価を認める　(l. 26) **heritage:** 遺産　(l. 27) **firsthand:** 直接に、じかに

《 Exercises 》

I Hear What You're Saying

1. The example of lighted castles is used to argue that the appearance of historical sites

- **a.** should basically stay unchanged over time.
- **b.** can change while showing respect for the past.
- **c.** has changed for the worse in modern times.

2. What does the writer say about the relationship between access and appearance?

- **a.** Finding a balance between access and historical appearance is an impossible goal.
- **b.** Slopes and handrails affect the appearance of historical buildings more than mats and tenji blocks do.
- **c.** Ease of access must sometimes be considered more important than preserving historical appearance.

3. Which of the following would the writer most likely agree with?

- **a.** Elevators have little affect on visitors' ability to appreciate the past.
- **b.** Castles should remind visitors of the past on both the outside and the inside.
- **c.** Concrete is the best material for recreating the atmosphere of the past.

Getting to the Point

1-61

Lydia: Once I hurt my leg in an accident and had to spend a couple of weeks in a wheelchair.

Nao: Oh? Did you have much trouble getting around?

Lydia: I'll say I did. Elevators are hard enough to find as it is, but my accident happened just before I went traveling. Some of the places I visited didn't have elevators at all, so I had to just sit there and wait outside.

Nao: That doesn't sound like much fun.

Lydia: Luckily, other places were completely barrier-free, so there I was able to enjoy myself with my friends. It gave us a lot to talk about afterward.

Nao: ( ). It's great when you can share an experience with your friends.

1. Draw a line under the word or expression in the passage that comes closest in meaning to the underlined part of the conversation.

2. Choose the best word or expression from those below to fill in the blank space in the conversation.

Good for you.	Happy to see you.	Best of luck to you.

3. Complete the following sentence by adding your own **supporting idea**.

I believe we need to improve barrier-free access because ______________

____

____.

Con

Possibilities and limitations

1-62

It's wishful thinking to imagine that going barrier-free will make everyone happy. I mean, it seems to me that when planners do try to make things barrier-free, they're only thinking of people in wheelchairs. They manage to improve access for one particular group, but that's where their planning stops, and they actually end up limiting access for others. I don't think that's what barrier-free is supposed to be about, even if a lot of people do benefit.

1-63

Take those wavy handrails that are supposed to help people climb up and down stairs. They're really only convenient for a small number of people, and everyone who finds a regular straight handrail more useful is being ignored, including people with disabilities. Or if a regular handrail is installed next to a wavy handrail, one of them will always be at an inconvenient height—and maybe both! Come up to one of these handrails while you're being carried along by the crowd and you come to a complete stop because it's not at all what you were expecting.

1-64

We can talk about changes to historical buildings, too. Suppose an elevator is installed in a castle made of wood. It's not just the elevator that has an effect. After all, people have to move around before getting on and after getting off. So other changes have to be made, and as a result, more and more damage is done to these historical treasures. The thing is, once the original is gone, the history is gone, too. That's why I don't visit concrete castles myself, and why I don't think we can make it possible for everyone to go absolutely everywhere. Instead of installing elevators, we should use high-quality video, audio guides, and even virtual reality to bring the experience to those who for one reason or another can't be given access.

Of course we can't ignore the problem of access, but we also can't ignore the fact that sometimes there's more to it than that.

《Notes》

(l. 1) **wishful thinking:** 希望的観測
(l. 6) **be about ~:** ～の本質である、～のあるべき姿である　(l. 8) **Take ~:** ～を例に取る
(l. 10) **regular:** 普通の、ありきたりの　(l. 13) **come up to ~:** ～に近付く、辿り着く
(l. 16) **suppose:** 仮定する　(l. 18) **after all:** 結局　(l. 21) **the original:** もとの物、原物
(l. 23) **absolutely:** 絶対に　(l. 25) **for one reason or another:** 何らかの理由で

《 Exercises 》

I Hear What You're Saying

1. What is one problem mentioned about barrier-free planning?

a. Those in wheelchairs are often ignored by barrier-free planners.
b. Helping one group sometimes creates problems for others.
c. Few people are actually helped by efforts to improve access.

2. Which of the following would the writer most likely agree with?

a. The best idea is to install both straight and wavy handrails.
b. Straight handrails should be replaced by wavy ones.
c. Wavy handrails are often placed at the wrong height.

3. The writer states that historical buildings such as castles

a. may not be high enough for elevators to be installed.
b. can lose their history when elevators are installed.
c. should offer videos and other media in their elevators.

Getting to the Point

1-65

Marina: Surprised to see me on crutches? I broke my ankle last week playing soccer.

Kai: That's tough. But lots of places are barrier-free now, so I imagine that makes things easier.

Marina: Hardly. I went to a museum yesterday, and all they had at the entrance was a slope up to the door. Regular stairs would have at least given me something flat to walk on. I had to watch my balance the whole time, and it was actually pretty scary.

Kai: I hadn't (   ). People think everything's just fine as long as a wheelchair can get through.

Marina: And benches—nobody seems to think about benches for people who need to sit down. I overheard some older people saying the same thing. I certainly could have used a bench yesterday.

Kai: Yeah, I can see where that might cause problems.

Marina: Sometimes I wish the planners would try a little harder to look beyond the obvious.

1. Draw a line under the word or expression in the passage that comes closest to having the opposite meaning of the underlined part of the conversation.

2. Choose the best word or expression from those below to fill in the blank space in the conversation.

attempted	realized	hesitated

3. Complete the following sentence by adding your own **opposing idea**.

One problem with barrier-free planning is that ______________________

____

____.

Elderly Drivers

Pro

Keep our seniors licensed

People need their own means of transportation to increase their range of movement. That goes for seniors, too. Age shouldn't be the only measure of how safe it is for them to keep their driver's licenses.

Let's think about what's good about letting elderly drivers continue driving. Everyone knows that keeping your mind and body active is important as you age. When seniors stop driving, they not only lose the chance to keep active, they can lose their sense of purpose in life. This lack of motivation can affect their mental attitude and even increase the speed of mental decline. Then more time has to be spent caring for them, which creates even more problems for our aging society. As a result, taking away their licenses doesn't seem logical to me.

But it's not only a matter of mental and physical health. In places where cars are the chief means of transport, being able to drive can be a matter of life and death for seniors. Seniors need their cars to go to work and get to the hospital. Stores can be far away from home, and there aren't many people or cars on the road to begin with, so safety doesn't really seem to be a major issue. Since having a car helps seniors stay independent, I don't really see much to worry about.

More and more places in Japan these days are graying rapidly, especially outside of the major cities. With public transportation either inconvenient to use or even nonexistent in these rural settings, it's only natural for seniors to own a car. We should think twice about making it mandatory for elderly drivers to return their licenses.

《 Notes 》

(Title) **elderly:** 年配の (l. 1) **means:** 手段 (l. 2) **that goes for ~:** ～についても言える
(l. 2) **senior:** 年配の方、高齢者 (l. 3) **driver's license:** 運転免許証
(l. 8) **mental attitude:** 精神的心構え (l. 9) **decline:** 衰え
(l. 11) **logical:** 合理的 (l. 13) **a matter of life and death:** 死活問題
(l. 19) **gray:** 高齢化する (l. 22) **mandatory:** 義務的な、強制的な

《 Exercises 》

I Hear What You're Saying

1. The writer seems to think that driving helps seniors by

a. improving the quality of care they receive.
b. making physical effort unnecessary in their lives.
c. giving them a feeling of being useful members of society.

2. Which of the following is NOT mentioned as an activity for which seniors need cars?

a. Going to visit friends.
b. Shopping at stores.
c. Driving to the hospital.

3. The writer suggests that the graying of Japan

a. will probably cause the number of trains and buses to increase.
b. is happening faster in the countryside than in the major cities.
c. means that more seniors want to return their driver's licenses.

Getting to the Point

2-04

Lydia: When I went back to see my family last month, I was sort of happy to see my grandpa was still doing a lot of driving.

Nao: Is there some reason he has to drive? Don't you think it's a little dangerous?

Lydia: Well, everyone else in the family works, so there's no one he can (   ) to drive him around. The supermarket is pretty far away, and he says he wants to make sure there are enough groceries and supplies in the house.

Nao: I get that. Older people aren't as strong as they used to be, and having a car makes it easier to carry lots of heavy things.

Lydia: Right, but he's still healthy enough to drive a car without any trouble. I think he'll be able to keep driving for quite a while yet.

Nao: Not much sense in making him stop just because he's reached a certain age, especially if his health's good and he needs the car in his daily life.

1. Draw a line under the word or expression in the passage that comes closest in meaning to the underlined part of the conversation.

2. Choose the best word or expression from those below to fill in the blank space in the conversation.

prepare for	argue with	depend on

3. Complete the following sentence by adding your own **supporting idea**.

I favor elderly drivers keeping their driver's licenses because ____________

____

____.

Con

Time to call it a day

2-05

Let's face it. Just because a minority of seniors can keep driving without causing an accident doesn't mean we should risk having more traffic accidents as a result. Elderly drivers have more accidents—no ifs, ands, or buts about it.

The undeniable truth is that physical and mental decline increases with age. With regard to driving, dementia is the problem most often mentioned in the news, but poor eyesight also affects driving skills, as does loss of hearing and the use of medication. The dangers of medication especially tend to be underestimated. Moreover, elderly people have slower reaction times, which makes it harder to deal with dangerous situations. Studies clearly show that the risk of having a fatal accident increases after the age of 75. Screening for dementia is all well and good, but right now the wait between tests is too long—driving skills are likely to change before a driver gets tested again. This gap makes it too easy to get overconfident, in my view.

2-06

Besides, the tests themselves are simple and unreliable. For example, you just get asked what day it is, or maybe you're supposed to remember what's in a drawing after the tester asks you a different question. You don't actually get tested on your knowledge of what drivers are expected to do out on the road. It's as though they're saying it's all right for your abilities to decline as long as you're not obviously affected by dementia.

2-07

Seniors don't even have to pass a behind-the-wheel test to keep their licenses. We have driving simulators now, so why not use those for testing? By all means, let's have more PR campaigns to make people aware of the increased danger of driving as we get older. But above all, I think we need to adopt a stricter approach to allowing seniors to hold on to their licenses.

《Notes》

(l. 1) **Let's face it.:** 素直に認めよう。 (l. 5) **undeniable:** 否定できない (l. 5) **decline:** 衰え
(l. 6) **dementia:** 認知症 (l. 8) **medication:** 医薬、薬 (l. 9) **tend to ~:** ～する傾向がある
(l. 9) **underestimate:** 過小評価する (l. 10) **reaction time:** 反応時間
(l. 11) **fatal accident:** 死亡事故 (l. 12) **screen:** 検査する、審査する
(l. 12) **well and good:** けっこうだ (l. 14) **overconfident:** 自信過剰の
(l. 16) **unreliable:** 信頼性のない、信頼できない
(l. 22) **behind-the-wheel:** 車上の；(車の) 実技の (l. 25) **above all:** 何よりも、とりわけ
(l. 26) **strict:** 厳しい、厳格な

《 Exercises 》

I Hear What You're Saying

1. What does the writer say about the effects of medication on elderly drivers?

a. Medication seems to affect driving less than poor eyesight does.
b. Dementia caused by medication is often reported in the media.
c. People tend to think medication is less dangerous than it really is.

2. Testing for dementia can lead to overconfidence because the tests

a. make drivers think their reaction time has become faster.
b. lead drivers to believe their skills have stayed at the same level.
c. force drivers to study hard before taking the tests.

3. Which of the following is mentioned as a problem for current dementia testing?

a. There are too many questions to answer.
b. The questions are too hard to answer.
c. The questions are too easy to answer.

Getting to the Point

2-08

Marina: My grandma just bought a new car. But it's her first time using an automatic transmission, so she says she's a little nervous.

Kai: But she still wants to keep driving?

Marina: Yep. The problem is, the car has all the latest hi-tech devices. She thought it would make things more convenient, but it's been (   ) to learn how to use them.

Kai: Didn't you say she was having some trouble with her legs?

Marina: Um-hm. That's one reason she bought the car, of course, but it also makes us think she's going to have problems operating it. We're really worried about her causing an accident. At least it has an automatic-braking system.

Kai: It almost sounds like you're expecting her to get into an accident.

Marina: Well, we <u>have mixed feelings about it</u>, that's for sure.

1. Draw a line under the word or expression in the passage that comes closest to having the opposite meaning of the underlined part of the conversation.

2. Choose the best word or expression from those below to fill in the blank space in the conversation.

challenging	gratifying	damaging

3. Complete the following sentence by adding your own **opposing idea**.

I believe it should be mandatory for elderly drivers to return their driver's licenses because ______________________________

____

______________________________.

School Clubs

Pro

Friends and fulfillment

2-09 Club activities are an essential part of school life that enrich and enhance it.

First of all, joining a club allows students to build relationships with students in different classes and different school years. School becomes more than just a place for taking classes—it becomes a place where you can interact with your peers, increasing your motivation and boosting self-confidence. Needless to say, this kind of social networking is an incredibly useful life skill. Moreover, by taking part in club-related events, contests, and other activities, the experience becomes something deeply personal and meaningful. You really get involved.

2-10 This sense of involvement includes more than just getting the chance to try something new. The activities take place right on the school grounds, meaning that students come to accept them as a normal part of eveyday life. It seems natural for them to go to the practice field or clubroom as soon as classes are over, which really lowers the bar as far as participation goes. No stressing over going to an unfamiliar place for the first time or wondering if you're going to fit in.

2-11 Besides, you can't find facilities for all these different activities just anywhere. If you live in an area without any local clubs or recreation grounds, you really appreciate the advantage of being able to take part in club activities at school. Just think of all the activities schools offer. Even in a big city, you'd never find so many local clubs in one place. Besides, you'd end up paying more for memberships in local clubs than you pay for club activities at school.

Schools should continue to take the lead in providing spaces where students can always find something new to challenge themselves. After all, education is more than just textbooks and the classroom. 25

《 Notes 》

(l. 1) **enhance:** 充実させる (l. 6) **interact with ~:** ～と交流する
(l. 6) **peer:** 同輩、同級生 (l. 6) **boost:** 高める、助長する
(l. 10) **involved:** （関心をもって）関わっている、（身近なものとして）参加している
(l. 14) **practice field:** 練習場 (l. 15) **lower the bar:** ハードルを下げる
(l. 16) **stress over ~:** ～にストレスを感じる (l. 16) **unfamiliar:** 不慣れな
(l. 17) **fit in:** なじむ、溶け込む (l. 20) **appreciate:** 高く評価する、有難みを感じる
(l. 25) **take the lead in ~:** 率先して～する、～の先端に立つ

《 Exercises 》

I Hear What You're Saying

1. By using the expression "get involved," the writer means that students in school clubs

a. start to take their regular school homework more seriously.
b. discover the personal and social benefits of being a member.
c. feel inspired to invite other classmates to join the club.

2. One benefit mentioned of having club activities on school grounds is that students

a. feel less stress because the surroundings are familiar.
b. are the only ones allowed to use school practice fields.
c. can finish club activities quickly and return home early.

3. What does the writer suggest concerning local clubs?

a. Membership is likely to cost more than taking part in school-club activities.
b. Such clubs are usually too crowded for students to use for school activities.
c. Big cities offer too many local clubs for students to choose wisely among them.

Getting to the Point

2-12

Lydia: You know, my junior high school had a flower-arrangement club for students.

Nao: That's unusual. So you were a member?

Lydia: For a while. There was a flower-arrangement teacher near my house who offered lessons, but I wasn't sure what I'd be getting into if I went there. Plus, I thought I'd be more comfortable with people close to my own age.

Nao: That makes sense. But you said "for a while." Does that mean you stopped going?

Lydia: Well, I stopped going to flower arrangement. But that doesn't mean I joined the go-straight-home-after-school club. (   ), I decided to go with a sports club. Since I came in late, it took me a little time to get up to speed. But I already knew everyone by sight, so that made it easier.

Nao: Wow, I'm jealous you had such a good experience with your club activities.

1. Draw a line under the word or expression in the passage that comes closest in meaning to the underlined part of the conversation.

2. Choose the best word or expression from those below to fill in the blank space in the conversation.

Furthermore	Nevertheless	Instead

3. Complete the following sentence by adding your own **supporting idea**.

I back participation in school clubs because ______________________________

____

____.

Con

Stress and frustration

2-13 In my opinion, it's much too easy for people to overlook the less attractive side of school clubs.

We can start with freedom—or rather the lack of it. School rules aren't supposed to apply once classes for the day have ended. But schools practically force students to take part in club activities, which keeps the students at school when many of them would rather be doing something else. The same goes for teachers. In addition to their regular teaching duties, they're assigned the responsibility of being club advisors. It's supposed to be voluntary, of course. But the pressure is usually too great to resist, even if some teachers are happy to do it.

2-14 Now, since advising is treated as a "voluntary" activity, no rules exist concerning work hours. That means that no matter how long teachers work, the schools don't have to pay them overtime. In other words, the teachers are essentially working for free, and any kind of work-life balance goes out the window. This sort of practice is far too common in Japan, and not just in schools. It's not normal, and the schools are basically getting away with breaking the law.

If schools can't afford to hire specialists, I think they should just do away with club activities. It certainly doesn't benefit students to have so many advisors who lack specialized knowledge or skills. I mean, sometimes the students know more about the activity than the faculty advisor does. And especially in the case of sports, if the advisor doesn't have some medical training, it can actually put the students in danger.

2-15 Supporters like to talk about convenience, but they're forgetting the needs of students who live a long way away from school. Practice in the morning, practice in the afternoon, practice on weekends—that can't be good either for the health or for studying. As for networking, well, you can't get a much smaller circle of contacts than the members of a school club. That's hardly what I'd call reaching out.

I think schools should devote more effort to supporting and cooperating with local clubs and other outside organizations. That kind of symbiosis is how they can create spaces for their students where expertise and safety come first.

《Notes》

(l. 4) **apply:** 適用される (l. 4) **practically:** 実質的に、半ば (l. 7) **regular:** 通常の
(l. 7) **duties:** 職務 (l. 8) **assign:** 任命する (l. 8) **voluntary:** 任意の
(l. 9) **resist:** 抵抗する (l. 11) **treat ~ as ~:** ～を～として取り扱う (l. 13) **overtime:** 残業手当
(l. 14) **essentially:** 実質的に (l. 14) **go out the window:** 消え失せる (l. 15) **practice:** 慣行
(l. 16) **get away with ~:** ～をやってのける (l. 18) **hire:** 雇う (l. 18) **specialist:** 専門家
(l. 27) **networking:** 人脈づくり (l. 30) **devote effort to ~:** ～に努力を注ぐ
(l. 31) **symbiosis:** 共生、共益 (l. 32) **expertise:** 専門技能、専門知識

《 Exercises 》

I Hear What You're Saying

1. One problem mentioned concerning school rules for students and teachers is that

a. students are expected to stay in school even after classes have ended.
b. teachers prefer to advise school clubs rather than teach regular classes.
c. students end up with no teachers to supervise their club activities.

2. According to the writer, the "voluntary" system of advising school clubs is unsatisfactory because

a. students in the clubs sometimes end up breaking the law.
b. schools rely too heavily on outside experts to supervise the students.
c. teachers lack the training needed to help keep students safe.

3. The writer criticizes the arguments of supporters of club activities by commenting on

a. the small number of social connections established by students in school clubs.
b. the limited amount of time students in clubs are given to practice after school.
c. the low rate of participation in clubs among students who live far from school.

Getting to the Point

2-16

Marina: Since the number of students is going down, the school abolished the club I was planning to join this year.

Kai: So they tell you to choose a club, then make it impossible to get into the one you wanted. Sheesh!

Marina: (   ), I'd rather spend my time doing something else. I think I'd get more out of it. If the school wants you to challenge yourself by trying something new, it doesn't make sense to take away the chance to do it.

Kai: Lots of us are only in clubs because we have to be, and on top of that, the clubs charge us to take part. It's the pits.

Marina: And the kids in clubs are really tight with each other, so if you get on somebody's wrong side, things can get a little tricky.

Kai: Yeah, whereas if you were just taking a class together, you could kind of shrug it off. I think they should let the ones who want to join a club go ahead and do it and leave the rest of us alone.

1. Draw a line under the word or expression in the passage that comes closest in meaning to the underlined part of the conversation.

2. Choose the best word or expression from those below to fill in the blank space in the conversation.

To be honest	To change the subject	To look on the bright side

3. Complete the following sentence by adding your own **opposing idea**.

I am not a fan of school clubs because ______________________________

____

____.

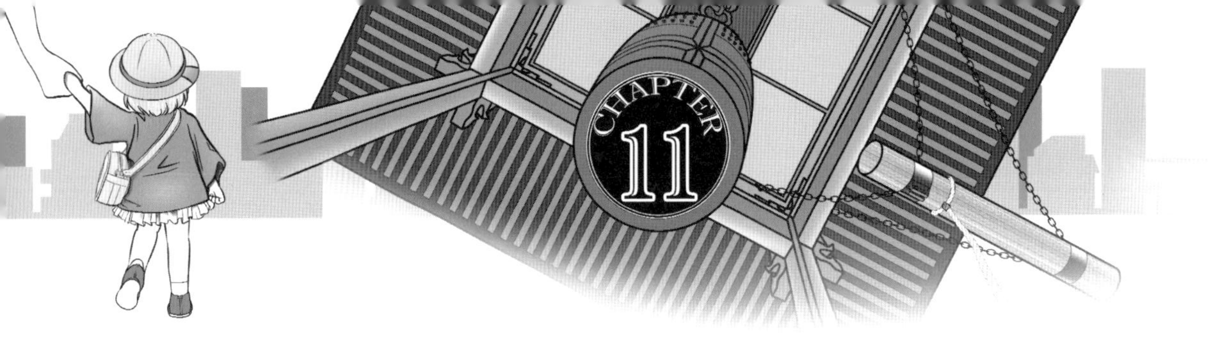

The NIMBY Syndrome

Pro

Welcome, neighbor

2-17 I have a hard time understanding why so many people say public and commercial facilities are just great... if they're built in some other location. For me, proximity is the whole point. That applies not only to places local residents can't avoid using—like city hall or the ward office—but also to supermarkets, convenience stores, and other commercial spots frequented 5 by residents and nonresidents alike. The upshot is that communities experience both economic benefits and a boost in the general quality of life.

2-18 I don't know about you, but having a hospital or fire station nearby puts my mind at ease regarding health problems and emergency situations. 10 Being able to count on a fast response when something goes wrong makes a big difference. In addition, our society has a growing number of working couples who are only too happy when there's a kindergarten or child-care center nearby. I mean, it's not as though these facilities hold noisy outdoor events every day, and besides, just how awful is it to have groups of little 15 children playing in the neighborhood?

2-19 Parks and other public spaces offer great opportunities for people of all ages to take part in local events. People feel less isolated and lonely in such an outgoing, lively environment, and they get to know who their neighbors are. A real community takes shape, with one of the side benefits 20 being less crime because neighbors are now looking out for each other.

It's true that traffic can increase as a result of commercial development, and there are real concerns about problems like light pollution and noise pollution. But these drawbacks are far outweighed by the concrete benefits of building active, diversified communities. 25

《 Notes 》

(Title) **NIMBY ("not in my backyard"):** 私の裏庭だけはやめてくれ；ニンビー
(Title) **syndrome:** 症候群　(l. 1) **public and commercial facilities:** 公共・商業施設
(l. 3) **proximity:** 近いこと　(l. 4) **city hall:** 市役所　(l. 4) **ward office:** 区役所
(l. 5) **frequent:** よく行く、よく出入りする　(l. 6) **upshot:** 結論、要点　(l. 7) **boost:** 増大
(l. 9) **put a person's mind at ease:** （人を）安心させる
(l. 11) **count on ~:** ～を頼りにする、～を当てにする　(l. 15) **awful:** ひどい
(l. 18) **isolated:** 孤立している　(l. 19) **outgoing:** 社交的な　(l. 23) **concern:** 懸念
(l. 24) **drawback:** 欠点　(l. 24) **concrete:** 具体的な　(l. 25) **diversified:** 多様な

《 Exercises 》

I Hear What You're Saying

1. Regarding public and commercial facilities, the writer argues that

a. public facilities should be replaced by commercial facilities.
b. nonresidents ought to pay for the facilities they use.
c. communities benefit from having a combination of both.

2. What does the writer suggest concerning child-care centers?

a. They are less important to quality of life than facilities like hospitals.
b. Working couples consider them a valuable part of neighborhood life.
c. Noise from the children is especially noticeable only at night.

3. Which of the following best expresses the writer's view of community events?

a. They should be held away from public places like parks.
b. They encourage residents to go and visit other neighborhoods.
c. They contribute to a reduction in the amount of crime.

Getting to the Point

Lydia: I just moved in, so I don't know the neighborhood very well yet, but when I was walking down the street, I met someone handing out flyers in front of a children's home.

Nao: Was something going on there?

Lydia: The children were putting on a show. They do it every year, apparently, and it's popular with everyone in the community. I had some time, so I decided to stop by and watch.

Nao: And how was it?

Lydia: It was fun! I never expected to have an experience like that in an area with so many stores and other businesses around. I made some new acquaintances and learned a lot more about my new neighborhood. It made me glad I decided to live in the area.

Nao: Sounds like a great place for those children to (   ), too.

1. Draw a line under the word or expression in the passage that comes closest in meaning to the underlined part of the conversation.

2. Choose the best word or expression from those below to fill in the blank space in the conversation.

3. Complete the following sentence by adding your own **supporting idea**.

Living close to public and commercial facilities is an advantage because

Con

Too far outside my comfort zone

2-21 People who don't live next to public facilities and commercial areas always talk about diversity and convenience. But I'd just like to remind them that they don't have the right to tell the rest of us what's good for us. They only see one side of things and ignore the fact that some people are paying a high price for that convenience. We're the ones living right next 5 to those facilities, you know—24/7!

2-22 Take child-care centers, for example. It's not just the problem of children being noisy. I mean, you've got the cars and bicycles of parents dropping their kids off and picking them up every single day, and those are pretty loud, too. You wonder if people who've never experienced it ever 10 give it a second thought. Commercial areas are jammed with delivery trucks that add vibration to the noise and air pollution they cause. There are so many pedestrian accidents and fender benders in my neighborhood now that I've started to be afraid of walking outside. At night, I've got bright headlights shining right into my window! 15

2-23 As for police and fire stations and hospitals, whenever they get a call for help, I have to put up with the sound of sirens wailing. Maybe I'm overreacting, but passing by hospitals filled with sick people makes me worry that my risk of catching an infection is going up. So it's like I'm balancing the possibility of getting sick against the convenience of having the hospital 20 so close if I have to be taken there myself.

What's more, I've never met most of the people I see in my neighborhood every day. I don't see how that's supposed to help prevent crime. In fact, I'm worried terrorists may consider us a soft target because nobody really knows anybody else. 25

Over and over, day after day—it's exhausting. I can definitely see the reason for having the expression "NIMBY."

《Notes》

(Title) **comfort zone:** 快感帯、快適ゾーン (l. 2) **remind:** 思い出させる、気づかせる
(l. 6) **24/7 (twenty-four seven):** 日 24 時間・週 7 日；四六時中
(l. 8) **drop ~ off:** ～を送り届ける (l. 9) **pick ~ up:** ～を迎えに来る
(l. 11) **jammed:** 混雑した (l. 12) **vibration:** 振動 (l. 13) **pedestrian:** 歩行者
(l. 13) **fender bender:** 軽度の交通事故 (l. 17) **put up with ~:** ～に我慢する、～に耐える
(l. 17) **wail:** 鳴り響く音 (l. 19) **infection:** 感染（症）
(l. 24) **soft target:** 防備の薄いところ、狙いやすい標的、軟目標

《 Exercises 》

I Hear What You're Saying

1. The writer uses the term "24/7" to express the idea that people who like to talk about diversity and convenience

a. spend too much of their time visiting public facilities and commercial areas.
b. spend very little of their time around public facilities and commercial areas.
c. spend most of their time criticizing public facilities and commercial areas.

2. One problem with child-care centers is said to be that

a. the vibrations from passing trucks frighten the children inside.
b. bicycles and cars increase the level of noise near the centers.
c. the centers' lights make it hard for nearby residents to sleep.

3. Why is the writer worried about not knowing many of the people in the neighborhood?

a. There may be terrorists pretending to be residents or visitors.
b. Friends say they are too tired to come and pay a visit.
c. Maybe no one will call the hospital if the writer falls ill.

Getting to the Point

2-24

Marina: I wish people would stop thinking I'm lonely or something just because I like being by myself. It's like they don't even stop to think about it.

Kai: You said it. Not everyone likes to take part in events and other activities.

Marina: I'm (   ) with strangers, so I find it really stressful to be surrounded by lots of people I don't know. I kind of have a panic attack even when I get stopped and asked for directions.

Kai: Same here. I like peace and quiet. Otherwise, I just want to stay inside more.

Marina: Not only that, there's so much cigarette smoke in the air now. And trash everywhere. Smells from exhaust fans and the hot air blowing out of the air-conditioner units—I could go on and on.

Kai: You don't want stores and things to be too far away, but it's a real headache when they're this close—and I mean that literally.

1. Draw a line under the word or expression in the passage that comes closest in meaning to the underlined part of the conversation.

2. Choose the best word or expression from those below to fill in the blank space in the conversation.

unreasonable	unpleasant	uncomfortable

3. Complete the following sentence by adding your own **opposing idea**.

I can sympathize with NIMBYists because ______________________________

____

____.

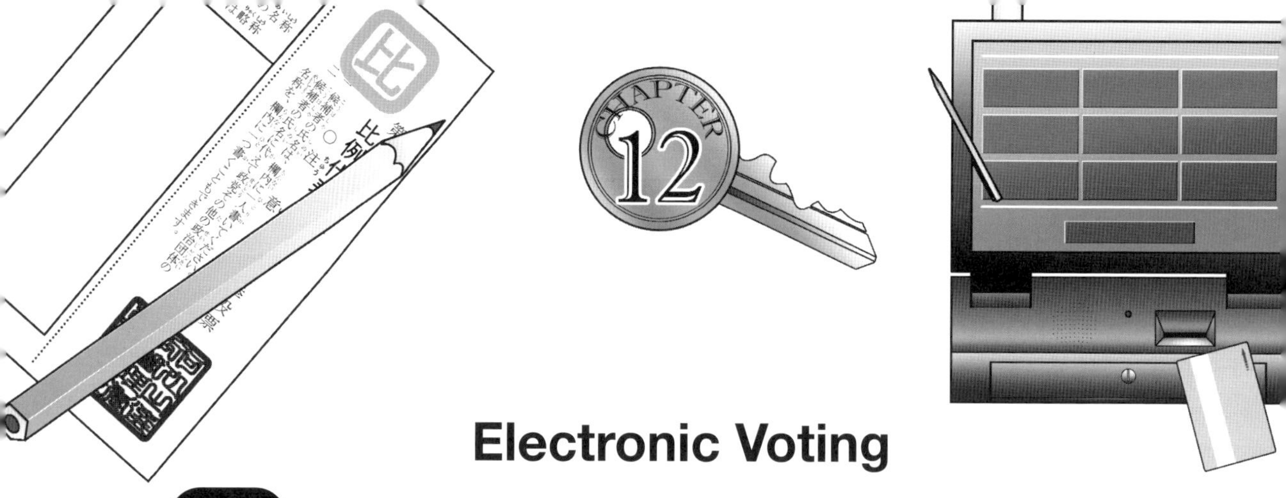

Electronic Voting

Pro

A win for democracy

Electronic voting is the only way we can expect voter turnout in Japan to get any better. Without it, I'm really worried about what will happen to democracy in this country.

Convenience is the key to getting people to vote in elections. Right now, though, the government isn't doing enough to make it easy for people to vote. It's true you can vote early if you can't get to the polls on election day and have a good reason. The trouble is, there aren't enough places where early voting is possible. And, of course, some people don't have the time to go anyway, while others have disabilities or chronic illnesses that prevent them from leaving home. With Japan's aging population, allowing electronic voting from home would eliminate a major barrier to making sure that citizens' voices are heard.

Electronic voting is convenient for regular voters, too. Using LED displays instead of paper for voting gives voters much more information and presents that information clearly. Photographs of the candidates can be shown, along with the names of their parties and their campaign promises. Voters can instantly tell who and what they're voting for. Electronic-voting machines can also be programmed to stop voters from making careless mistakes—for example, no accidental votes for more than one candidate. The votes can be counted automatically in real time, with no extra effort needed to ignore blank ballots. All of the time-consuming problems of traditional voting can be avoided by switching to electronic voting.

The ease and efficiency of electronic voting make it a clear winner in the effort to increase participation in the political process.

《 Notes 》

(l. 1) **(voter) turnout:** （選挙の）投票者数　(l. 6) **get to the polls:** 投票場へ行く
(l. 9) **chronic illness:** 慢性病、持病　(l. 11) **eliminate:** 取り除く
(l. 11) **make sure that ~:** ～を確実にする　(l. 12) **citizen:** 市民、国民
(l. 16) **campaign promise:** 公約　(l. 18) **program:** プログラミングする
(l. 21) **blank ballot:** 白票　(l. 21) **time-consuming:** 時間のかかる、手間取る
(l. 22) **switch:** 切り替える　(l. 24) **political process:** 政治過程

《 Exercises 》

I Hear What You're Saying

1. One problem mentioned about early voting is that

a. the government charges citizens a fee to vote early.
b. disabilities may prevent citizens from leaving the house.
c. the places where citizens can vote are dangerously old.

2. What is said to be an advantage of display screens?

a. They make voting seem like playing a video game.
b. They show information in an easy-to-understand way.
c. They are inexpensive because they use so little electricity.

3. The writer says that switching to electronic voting would save time because

a. blank ballots could easily be found and removed.
b. there would be no need to announce the results.
c. votes would be counted for just one candidate.

Getting to the Point

2-28

Lydia: I don't believe it—rain pouring down like this on election day. Maybe we should just stay home.

Nao: It makes you realize how convenient electronic voting would be.

Lydia: I wonder how many other people the bad weather's going to keep away.

Nao: Well, don't let that influence you. You're the one who's always complaining about how awful the government's policies are. You've got to get out and vote if you want <u>to make a difference</u>.

Lydia: Yeah, yeah, I know. I already feel guilty about not going last time, when I had that awful headache. I could have voted then if we'd had online voting.

Nao: Um-hm. You could have sent in your vote with ( ). That way, you could forget all about the weather.

1. Draw a line under the word or expression in the passage that comes closest in meaning to the underlined part of the conversation.

2. Choose the best word or expression from those below to fill in the blank space in the conversation.

the flip of a coin	the tap of a finger	the spark of an idea

3. Complete the following sentence by adding your own **supporting idea**.

I am happy with the idea of electronic voting because ____________________

____

____.

Con

I vote no

2-29

Despite the convenience, there are just too many drawbacks for electronic voting to be workable.

For one thing, since the voting process is so important, the underlying computer system needs to be rock solid. But as we all know, computer systems always have bugs in their programming. In addition, the election workers all have to be trained to use the computers. Who's going to do that? As long as humans are the ones who program and operate the system, human error will never be completely eliminated. One little slip is all it takes for your personal information to leak out into cyberspace, and something like that could affect tens of thousands of voters—or more. Once that genie gets out of the bottle, you can't put it back again.

2-30

Then there's the challenge of protecting against outside attacks. The news is full of stories about attempts by hackers, crackers, and government spies to influence elections. How are we going to guarantee the security of the system against these invisible intruders? I seriously doubt supporters have given that much consideration. At least with analog voting, you can restrict access to real live people, and for security you only really need strong locks and sharp eyes. No programming skills required, and you can save on costs, too. It may seem ironic, but in that respect analog is more efficient than digital. And you certainly don't have to hire specialists to repair and maintain the equipment, or find a special place to store it.

High risk, low return. That's the story when it comes to electronic voting.

《 Notes 》

(l. 1) **despite ~:** ～にもかかわらず　(l. 1) **drawback:** 難点、欠点
(l. 3) **underlying:** 基礎をなす　(l. 4) **rock solid:**（石のように）堅固な、絶対安定した
(l. 9) **leak:** 漏れる　(l. 11) **genie:** 精霊；（ひいては）厄介ごと
(l. 11) **the genie gets out of the bottle:** だれにも止められない
(l. 13) **hacker:** ハッカー、コンピュータ技術に通じている人
(l. 13) **cracker:** クラッカー、コンピュータ技術に通じてそれを悪用しようとする人
(l. 15) **intruder:** 侵入者　(l. 17) **restrict:** 制限する、限定する　(l. 19) **ironic:** 皮肉な
(l. 21) **equipment:** 設備、機器

《 Exercises 》

I Hear What You're Saying

1. According to the writer, one shortcoming with computer systems is that

a. humans can make mistakes operating them.
b. the systems need large amounts of electricity to work.
c. election workers want to use the computers at home.

2. The image of a genie in a bottle is used to explain the risk that comes from

a. too many people trying to vote at the same time.
b. voters' personal data getting leaked into cyberspace.
c. accidentally damaging computers while using them.

3. The writer prefers analog voting over digital voting because

a. hackers are confused by how analog equipment works.
b. digital equipment needs to be replaced regularly.
c. analog equipment is more secure than digital equipment.

Getting to the Point

2-31

Marina: This is the first time they've allowed online voting, but I don't have any idea what I'm doing. Could I ask you to vote instead of me?

Kai: Don't they check somehow to make sure it's really you?

Marina: Just a password. I've got it right here. (   ) you vote for the person I tell you to, there shouldn't be any problem.

Kai: Well, but does that make it right? It would be pretty easy for me to vote for a different candidate if I really wanted to.

Marina: But what do they expect you to do if you can't make it to a polling station and need help getting connected and stuff?

Kai: <u>It looks like they didn't think the process through very well</u>. I have the feeling that the number of voters isn't going to change very much.

1. Draw a line under the word or expression in the passage that comes closest in meaning to the underlined part of the conversation.

2. Choose the best word or expression from those below to fill in the blank space in the conversation.

As long as	As free as	As much as

3. Complete the following sentence by adding your own **opposing idea**.

I am not willing to go along with electronic voting because ____________

____

____.

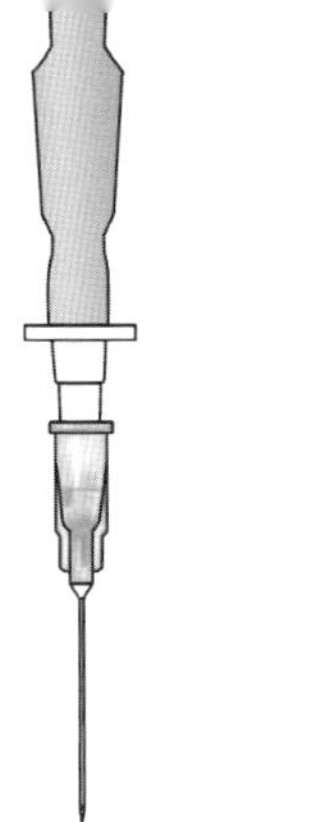

Aid in Dying

Pro

My life, my decision

If I have the right to live my life, don't I also have the right to decide when to end it? As long as no one else is harmed, I think the decision to die should be considered a human right like any other.

The only thing that really matters is getting a person's consent. Letting someone die by switching off the person's life support is already common in a lot of countries. This widely accepted form of ending life is called "passive euthanasia." Another form of aid in dying is "assisted suicide," which is permitted in parts of North America and Europe. This is when a doctor or some other person provides life-ending drugs to a person who has only a short time to live and is in great pain. Five countries—including the Netherlands, Belgium, and Canada—allow a doctor or some other person to go one step further and administer drugs directly to a person who wants to die. In other words, even this kind of "active euthanasia" is legal now, and rightly so from my point of view. Courts hardly ever accept challenges to such decisions.

The single serious issue comes when doctors agree that a person can't live much longer and is suffering unbearable pain, but for some reason the person can't give consent. Are we supposed to just stand around and watch the person suffer, even though death is certain and freedom from pain is so easy to provide? I take the position that even in such cases, a doctor should be allowed to administer life-ending drugs directly without fear of any legal problems coming up later.

Making people suffer isn't protecting their human rights. Helping them find release from pain is what makes death with dignity possible.

《 Notes 》

(Title) **aid in dying:** 安楽死させること；安楽死　(l. 4) **consent:** 同意、承諾
(l. 7) **passive euthanasia:** 消極的安楽死　(l. 7) **suicide:** 自殺
(l. 12) **administer:** 与える；施す　(l. 13) **active euthanasia:** 積極的安楽死
(l. 14) **court:** 裁判所　(l. 14) **challenge:** 異議を申し立てる
(l. 24) **death with dignity:** 尊厳死

《 Exercises 》

I Hear What You're Saying

1. Which of the following is said to be true about assisted suicide?

a. It is permitted in places for those in great pain.
b. It is currently available only in Europe.
c. It means turning off patients' life-support machines.

2. Which of the following is said to be true about active euthanasia?

a. Courts usually try to prevent it from happening.
b. The person who wants to die must take the drugs him- or herself.
c. It is legal in a relatively small number of countries.

3. The "serious issue" mentioned by the writer is one that concerns

a. passive euthanasia.
b. assisted suicide.
c. active euthanasia.

Getting to the Point

2-34

Lydia: I've got a friend who's had serious health problems for years. She and her family have been going through endless stress and suffering.

Nao: That sounds heartbreaking. I imagine their medical costs must be high, too.

Lydia: Yeah, apparently. She says she doesn't have any hope for the future, so she wishes she could find someone to help her die.

Nao: How can she say something that? It's so final. I think she ought to keep on going, no matter what.

Lydia: Are you volunteering to take care of her, then? Wouldn't it be better if she could die peacefully, surrounded by the ones she loves? (   ), the only path open to her might be suicide. That would be a real tragedy.

Nao: Hmm, it looks like I should have given it more thought before I spoke. Maybe I need to try harder to see it <u>from her perspective</u>.

1. Draw a line under the word or expression in the passage that comes closest in meaning to the underlined part of the conversation.

2. Choose the best word or expression from those below to fill in the blank space in the conversation.

Similarly	Otherwise	Regardless

3. Complete the following sentence by adding your own **supporting idea**.

I am a supporter of aid in dying because ______________________________

____

____.

Con

Where do we draw the line?

2-35

Some ideas are simply unworkable regardless of the good intentions behind them. That's how it is with aid in dying, especially assisted suicide and active euthanasia.

My view is that no one is qualified to set the standards for deciding whether someone should live or die. Passing a law isn't enough, even assuming that passing a law is possible. In fact, a law regulating assisted dying might even end up increasing the suicide rate. That's because laws can create unconscious pressure, lowering the barriers against committing suicide. That kind of risk needs to be taken into account. People who get sick and want to kill themselves might take the easy way out by using the law to end their lives legally—even when they could be treated successfully. Or consider the problem of consent. Who determines the age at which someone is old enough to end their own life? Are you confident you could decide in that person's place?

2-36

All I'm saying is that standards are necessarily subjective in nature. Another case in point is judging people's mental condition. How are we supposed to measure the level of a person's hope for the future? Where is the borderline between making a rational decision to die and deciding as a result of depression caused by a mental disorder? I'm absolutely certain that some disturbed individuals would refuse treatment and make themselves sicker just so they could end their lives legally. Or a doctor might lie to a family about how serious a patient's illness is—even when there's the possibility of keeping the patient alive until a cure can be found. The doctor thinks that helping the person die would make things easier for the family, and the family believes the doctor's lie. It's terrifying.

In the end, the line between euthanasia and murder is too thin for any human being to draw—especially when no one can predict what the future might hold.

《Notes》

(l. 1) **unworkable:** 実行不可能な　(l. 1) **good intentions:** 善意　(l. 4) **standard:** 基準
(l. 5) **assume that ~:** ～と仮定して　(l. 6) **regulate:** 規定する
(l. 8) **commit suicide:** 自殺する　(l. 9) **take ~ into account:** ～を考慮に入れる
(l. 12) **determine:** 決定する　(l. 16) **case in point:** 適例
(l. 18) **rational:** 理性的、合理的　(l. 19) **depression:** 憂うつ、うつ病
(l. 19) **mental disorder:** 精神障害　(l. 20) **disturbed:** 神経症の、精神障害のある
(l. 23) **cure:** 治療（法）　(l. 27) **what the future holds:** 将来何が起こるか、将来のこと

《 Exercises 》

I Hear What You're Saying

1. The writer argues that suicide rates might increase under an assisted-dying law because

a. the law would pay the costs for those who decide to end their lives.
b. medical treatment would not be given to those who want to end their lives.
c. people might think the law makes ending their lives seem like a good choice.

2. Which of the following is NOT mentioned as an example of subjective standards?

a. Deciding how long individuals must wait before choosing to end their lives.
b. Deciding the mental condition of individuals who want to end their lives.
c. Deciding the age at which individuals can choose to end their lives.

3. The possibility of a doctor lying to a family is terrifying to the writer because it means that

a. the doctor wants to increase the family's suffering.
b. patients might die despite the chance of being saved.
c. the family will refuse to believe what the doctor tells them.

Getting to the Point

2-37

Marina: When you think about it, filling out an organ-donor card is pretty scary. People change their minds all the time, but if an accident happens or you fall into a coma and can't say anything, then what?

Kai: Well, an organ-donor card is <u>the objective standard of proof</u> doctors can use to decide. Besides, what if the doctors are sure you're not going to survive?

Marina: They only know what medicine can do today. Who can tell what's going to happen in the future?

Kai: You mean like what if a new kind of drug is invented or something?

Marina: Exactly. And even if it doesn't cure you, it could reduce the pain or at least help you move around freely.

Kai: So you're saying (   ) to give up hope.

Marina: That's right—there's no room for regret once you're dead and gone.

1. Draw a line under the word or expression in the passage that comes closest to having the opposite meaning of the underlined part of the conversation.

2. Choose the best word or expression from those below to fill in the blank space in the conversation.

it doesn't pay	it can't hurt	it won't matter

3. Complete the following sentence by adding your own **opposing idea**.

I stand against aid in dying because ________________________________

____

____.

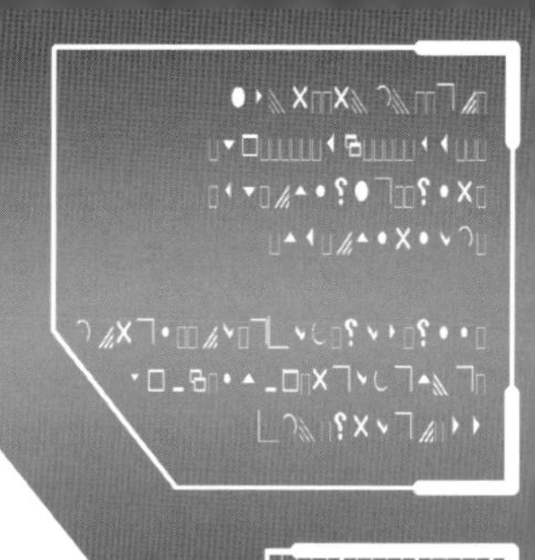

Biometric Authentication

Pro

The real deal

2-38 Biometric authentication is a cutting-edge method of providing effortless security. It's like a lock that can only be opened with information provided by a single individual. That person—and only that person—has the key. It's the most secure form of protection you can have.

Photographs in passports and on driver's licenses are often used for identification, but of course people don't always look like their photographs. Over time they gain or lose weight, they get older, and sometimes they fall ill. Just think how you looked in *your* last passport photo. Authentication becomes much more accurate when biological characteristics are used instead: fingerprint scanning, for example, or scanning your irises or the vein patterns in your hand. These characteristics don't change over time, so they're far more reliable than photographs. In a rapidly aging society like ours, biometric authentication can be called an ideal method of verification.

2-39 Medical treatment is the perfect example of how biometrics provide both security and safety while improving efficiency. Once a patient's information is digitized, medical professionals can share it with colleagues at hospitals or other facilities, making it easy to provide prompt and appropriate treatment to the same person wherever he or she may go. Sharing only works because the patient is actually there. No cases of mistaken identity, and no one has to memorize any passwords—because they don't exist!

2-40 Companies benefit no less. How much time do companies spend entering passwords for their employees, then reentering or resetting them when the passwords are forgotten? With biometrics, all that time and expense becomes a thing of the past. Customer service improves, too, since repeat customers who use voice verification, for example, can have their records accessed automatically when they log in—no need for employees to waste time searching for their files. Oh, and needless to say, with biometrics there's no language barrier to get in the way.

Biometric authentication used to be the stuff of science-fiction movies, but now I think it's fair to say it's ready for mainstream use. 30

《 Notes 》

(l. 1) **biometric authentication:** 生体認証　(l. 1) **cutting-edge:** 最先端
(l. 1) **effortless:** 努力を要しない、簡単な
(l. 9) **biological characteristics:** 生物学的特性　(l. 10) **iris:** 虹彩
(l. 10) **vein pattern:** 静脈［血管］パターン　(l. 12) **reliable:** 信頼できる
(l. 13) **verification:** 検証、照合　(l. 15) **efficiency:** 能率　(l. 16) **digitize:** デジタル化
(l. 16) **medical professionals:** 医療関係者　(l. 16) **colleague:** 同僚
(l. 17) **prompt:** 迅速な、素早い　(l. 17) **appropriate:** 適切な
(l. 24) **repeat customer:** リピート客　(l. 29) **the stuff of ~:** ～の題材
(l. 30) **fair to say ~:** ～と言っても正しい、～と言える　(l. 30) **mainstream:** 主流の

《 Exercises 》

I Hear What You're Saying

1. One problem mentioned with using photographs for ID is that

a. many people do not have passports or driver's licenses.
b. the appearance of the person in the photograph can change.
c. the colors in the photograph start to fade over time.

2. Biometrics are said to be helpful for medical treatment because

a. patient data can be shared securely by different facilities.
b. digitizing the data only takes place after treatment has finished.
c. medical professionals remember all the necessary passwords.

3. According to the writer, companies benefit from biometrics because

a. their customers no longer need to contact customer service very often.
b. they can avoid the work of entering and resetting passwords.
c. their employees can learn to speak different foreign languages.

Getting to the Point

2-41

Lydia: I can't believe I used to spend so much time typing in passwords. Now fingerprint scanning and facial recognition make logging in practically (   ).

Nao: At first I was skeptical biometrics would work very well, but I have to admit the accuracy is pretty amazing. I use the hand scanners at the bank all the time.

Lydia: I could never deal with remembering lots of passwords, so I ended up just using the same one over and over.

Nao: That really <u>increases your vulnerability</u>. Biometrics are so much more secure.

Lydia: Yeah. You can't fake it from a distance, either—the person always has to be right there.

Nao: It certainly solves the problem of not being able to log in because you forgot your PIN or password.

1. Draw a line under the word or expression in the passage that comes closest to having the opposite meaning of the underlined part of the conversation.

2. Choose the best word or expression from those below to fill in the blank space in the conversation.

instantaneous	premature	unpredictable

3. Complete the following sentence by adding your own **supporting idea**.

I am convinced of the value of biometrics because ____________________

____

____.

Con

A false sense of security

2-42

Biometric authentication isn't really any more secure than using traditional passwords. Security is something you should never take for granted.

You might think you're protected because your biological characteristics are private, but you'd be wrong. Private? Has anyone ever managed to go through life hiding their eyes, their hands, or their behavior? The internet is flooded with photos and videos. Anything you've ever held in your hand has left fingerprints behind. It's no different from pasting sticky notes with your password on them everywhere you go. The easier technology makes it to take high-resolution photos and the like, the less secure biometric authentication becomes.

2-43

Effective methods of faking biometric authentication already exist. As a result, the systems can be cracked even without the individual there to touch or operate them. Channels have been set up online for selling leaked data, and once yours has been sold, there's nothing you can do to change data based on your own body. Game over, my friend.

Here's something else they don't tell you: voiceprints, electrocardiograms (ECGs), fingerprints, vein recognition, keyboard typing patterns—they're all unique to an individual, but they do change over time. So if you find out one day that your biometrics won't work, it's a real pain to re-register them. It's a lot more trouble than just changing your password. Instead of locking out other people, your unique biology now locks you out, too. Ironic, isn't it?

2-44

If your own biometrics don't work, then it's back to using passwords. But that means companies always have to keep a backup system in place, ready to go. It's doubtful whether they save any time or money that way. Sure, passwords get stolen, but passwords can always be changed or reset. If your biometrics get stolen, you've lost that particular key for the rest of your life. That's hardly what I'd call secure.

《Notes》

(l. 1) **traditional:** 従来の　(l. 2) **take ~ for granted:** ～を当たり前のこと思いこむ
(l. 7) **paste:** 貼る　(l. 7) **sticky note:** 付箋　(l. 9) **high-resolution:** 高解像度、ハイレゾ
(l. 9) **the like:** その他同類のもの、～など　(l. 11) **fake:** 偽造する
(l. 12) **crack:** クラックする　(l. 13) **channel:** 経路、ルート
(l. 14) **leaked:** 漏洩された　(l. 17) **vein recognition:** 静脈認証
(l. 17) **typing pattern:** タイピング・パターン；キーボードへの打ち込みの特徴
(l. 19) **a pain:** 悩みの種、一苦労　(l. 22) **ironic:** 皮肉な　(l. 25) **doubtful:** 疑わしい、怪しい
(l. 27) **that particular:** その特定の、その

《 Exercises 》

I Hear What You're Saying

1. One reason mentioned for doubting the level of privacy in biometric authentication is that

a. technology makes it increasingly easy to access someone else's biometrics.
b. biological characteristics are actually shared by large numbers of people.
c. photographs and fingerprints have long been successful at protecting privacy.

2. The writer uses the expression "game over" to suggest that individuals cannot

a. crack authentication systems based on biometric data.
b. find places to sell their biometric data online.
c. change their biometric data after it has been leaked.

3. Which of the following is NOT mentioned as an additional problem of using biometric authentication?

a. Re-registering biometric data is more troublesome than resetting passwords.
b. Individuals have trouble understanding how biometric authentication works.
c. Companies lose time and money maintaining backup authentication systems.

Getting to the Point

2-45

Marina: I tried to do a fingerprint scan the other day, but the scanner wouldn't recognize my finger. It turns out my prints aren't clear enough anymore.

Kai: Is it because you handle all those chemicals at work?

Marina: Yeah, that seems to be the reason. So they wanted me to switch to iris scanning, but I wear color contacts, so that idea went nowhere.

Kai: I can't believe they didn't plan ahead for something like that.

Marina: Well, it does make you wonder how they can use reliability as (   ) depending on biometrics.

Kai: It's like forcing you use exactly the same password for everything you do—only you can't change it. <u>It's practically the opposite of</u> strong security.

1. Draw a line under the word or expression in the passage that comes closest to having the opposite meaning of the underlined part of the conversation.

2. Choose the best word or expression from those below to fill in the blank space in the conversation.

a complaint about	an attack on	an excuse for

3. Complete the following sentence by adding your own **opposing idea**.

I object to using biometric authentication because ______________________

____

____.

Animal Testing

Pro

A price worth paying

Testing on animals is essential to ensure the safety of commercial products and, more importantly, for the development of medical research.

Scientists and doctors have developed large numbers of life-saving drugs and treatments thanks to animal testing. Testing on chimpanzees, for example, gave us an effective polio vaccine, and insulin was discovered as a result of experiments on the pancreases of dogs. Testing is especially useful when it involves animals whose genetic makeup resembles that of humans. For instance, the hepatitis B vaccine wouldn't have existed without testing on chimpanzees, which share about 99 percent of their DNA with humans. Even mice share as much as 98 percent of their DNA with humans, so they're considered indispensable to cancer research.

Living subjects are necessary for experiments because tissue cultures alone don't allow scientists to study the complex changes that take place inside the body. In addition, the life cycles of animals are shorter than those of humans, meaning that effects can be studied over an entire lifetime or even over several generations. Shorter lifespans also mean studies can be conducted quickly, which brings in more funding from government organizations. As a result, medical science can move forward at a fairly rapid pace.

Concern over animal testing understandably centers on suffering. This is why many countries have passed laws to make sure the animals are treated humanely. Of course, cruelty has no place in animal testing. But most scientists recognize the need for such testing because of the benefits to human beings. It's also worth mentioning that animals themselves often benefit from this kind of testing.

Consider this: many more animals die to provide people with food than are sacrificed for medical research. If you don't object to eating meat, how can you object to humane testing that is equally important to keeping us healthy? When all is said and done, if it comes down to a choice between the welfare of human beings or the welfare of animals, I go with the former. 30

《 **Notes** 》

(l. 1) **ensure:** 確保する　(l. 5) **vaccine:** ワクチ　(l. 5) **insulin:** インスリン
(l. 6) **pancreas:** 膵臓　(l. 7) **genetic makeup:** 遺伝子構造
(l. 7) **resemble:** 類似する、～に似ている　(l. 8) **hepatitis B:** B型肝炎
(l. 11) **indispensable:** 必要不可欠　(l. 12) **tissue culture:** 組織培養
(l. 16) **generation:** 世代　(l. 17) **conduct:** 実施する、行う　(l. 17) **funding:** 助成金
(l. 20) **concern:** 懸念　(l. 22) **humanely:** 人道的に　(l. 22) **cruelty:** 残酷さ、虐待
(l. 23) **recognize:** 認める、承認する　(l. 27) **sacrifice:** 犠牲にする　(l. 30) **welfare:** 福祉
(l. 31) **former:** 前者

《 Exercises 》

I Hear What You're Saying

1. According to the writer, a vaccine for hepatitis B was

a. produced from the DNA of mice.
b. created from an effective polio vaccine.
c. developed from testing on chimpanzees.

2. One reason given for the need for live subjects is that

a. government organizations realize that good research takes time.
b. complex changes are hard to study through the use of tissue cultures.
c. humans and animals both enjoy life cycles of about the same length.

3. Regarding suffering, the writer suggests that animals

a. do not actually experience pain during testing.
b. can be tested without being cruel to them.
c. understand the sacrifice they are making.

Getting to the Point

2-49

Lydia: It's scary to think of using a medicine that hasn't been tested on animals.

Nao: My thoughts exactly. A drug may seem effective in a Petri dish, but that doesn't mean it's going to be safe for humans.

Lydia: You said it. Using a medicine without testing it on animals is no different from experimenting directly on people.

Nao: And an untested medicine could even cause the symptoms to get worse. Not to (   ) the risk of side-effects.

Lydia: Safe medicines have to be developed quickly, and that won't happen unless we have animal testing.

Nao: Ultimately, people shouldn't have to die so that we can protect animals.

1. Draw a line under the word or expression in the passage that comes closest in meaning to the underlined part of the conversation.

2. Choose the best word or expression from those below to fill in the blank space in the conversation.

mention	disturb	question

3. Complete the following sentence by adding your own **supporting idea**.

I accept that animal testing is necessary because ______________________

____

____.

Con

Senseless cruelty

2-50 Let me be clear about this—animal testing is a cruel practice that only benefits human beings.

The only real way to demonstrate the long-term effects of drugs on humans is for them to be used on humans. Common sense, no? Thanks to past testing, for example, we already know a lot about the safety of most of the active ingredients used in cosmetics. So companies only need to continue to use those ingredients to manufacture new products. As far as I can see, the only reason for companies to conduct any new testing on animals is greed—to get a head start on developing new active ingredients to bring to market. It's the worst kind of profit-first motivation.

2-51 Animal testing isn't even all that reliable. No matter how similar their genetic information may be, the plain fact is that animals and humans are different types of living creatures. To get technical about it, for example, research has been done comparing chromosome 22 in both humans and chimpanzees. That research has identified about a 5 percent difference in the genome's base sequence—but a difference of more than 80 percent in the genes created from that sequence. Similar base sequence, different genes. As a result, 94 percent of the medicines successfully tested on animals have failed in clinical trials on human beings. That's the reason why we still don't have an effective HIV vaccine.

2-52 On the other hand, some drugs are harmful to animals but effective in humans. This suggests that relying too much on animal testing may be causing us to overlook the benefits of these other drugs to humans. What purpose is there to testing animals when there's so much we might be missing? Instead, we keep the animals locked up in disgraceful conditions, rubbing creams into their skin—or worse—until their bodies have been ravaged. Then, as soon as they've served their purpose, we put them down.

The treatment of test animals under any conditions is truly cruel and inhumane, but mostly it gets swept under the rug. The stories that do sometimes make it into the news are only the tip of the iceberg. Maybe in the past there weren't any alternatives to testing on animals. But those alternatives exist today. As a result, we can't act fast enough to stop this shameful practice. 30

《Notes》

(l. 6) **active ingredient:** 有効成分　(l. 9) **greed:** 貪欲　(l. 9) **head start:** 有利なスタート
(l. 9) **bring ~ to market:** ~を市場に出す　(l. 11) **reliable:** 信頼性のある
(l. 13) **To get technical about it:** 技術的に言えば　(l. 14) **chromosome:** 染色体
(l. 16) **genome:** ゲノム　(l. 16) **base sequence:** 塩基配列　(l. 19) **clinical trial:** 臨床実験
(l. 25) **disgraceful:** 不名誉な、はしたない　(l. 27) **ravage:** 荒らす、ボロボロにする
(l. 27) **serve one's purpose:** 目的にかなう、役割を果たす　(l. 27) **put down:** 殺処分する
(l. 29) **sweep ~ under the rug:** ~を隠す、うやむやにする　(l. 31) **alternative:** 選択肢
(l. 32) **shameful:** 恥ずべく、けしからぬ

《 Exercises 》

I Hear What You're Saying

1. The writer suggests that companies continue to rely on animal testing because they

a. are especially concerned about the safety of human beings.
b. think that new active ingredients will make more money for them.
c. have found that animal testing costs less than testing on humans.

2. What is the key point made by the writer about the scientific research on chromosomes?

a. The research proves that the base sequences of chimpanzees and humans are very different.
b. The research shows that the development of an effective HIV vaccine is not far away.
c. The research demonstrates that the reliability of genetic studies can be questioned.

3. The writer objects to relying too heavily on animal testing because

a. drugs that are harmful to animals may actually benefit human beings.
b. poor living conditions change the effects of drugs on animals.
c. the animals being tested start to feel lonely and depressed.

Getting to the Point

2-53

Marina: Recently, lots of cosmetics have labels that say "Not tested on animals." In vivo testing, I think that sort of testing is called—testing on living things.

Kai: Really? Are the cosmetics safe?

Marina: They use something called in vitro testing, which means they don't need live animals.

Kai: How do they do that? What do they use instead of animals?

Marina: Well, they can actually grow artificial human skin out of skin cells, or they use plant protein or bacteria. It's done in Petri dishes and test tubes and stuff, like a science experiment. "In vitro" actually means "in glass," you know.

Kai: In vivo, in vitro—they sound alike, but I guess it's a big difference.

Marina: They can even use computers now to (   ) how drugs work in the human body. That's called in silico testing because computers only need silicon chips to run.

Kai: So if they can do it with the weather, they can do it with people, huh? Well, if we have those other methods, we might as well use products that don't get tested on animals. That certainly seems <u>to be the right thing to do</u>.

1. Draw a line under the word or expression in the passage that comes closest to having the opposite meaning of the underlined part of the conversation.

2. Choose the best word or expression from those below to fill in the blank space in the conversation.

defend	reduce	predict

3. Complete the following sentence by adding your own **opposing idea**.

   I object strongly to animal testing because ________________________________

   ____

   ____.

議論伯仲：ふたつの意見

検印
省略

© 2020年1月31日　初版発行
2024年1月31日　第2刷発行

著　者　Mark Jewel

発行者　小川　洋一郎

発行所　株式会社　朝日出版社
101-0065　東京都千代田区西神田 3-3-5
電話　東京　(03) 3239-0271/72
FAX　東京　(03) 3239-0479
e-mail　text-e@asahipress.com
振替口座　00140-2-46008
組版／クロス・コンサルティング　製版／錦明印刷

乱丁・落丁はお取り替えいたします。
ISBN978-4-255-15647-7　C1082